CLASSICS IN EDUCATION
Lawrence A. Cremin, General Editor

☆　　☆　　☆

THE REPUBLIC AND THE SCHOOL
Horace Mann on the Education of Free Men
Edited by Lawrence A. Cremin

AMERICAN IDEAS ABOUT ADULT EDUCATION
1710-1951
Edited by C. Hartley Grattan

DEWEY ON EDUCATION
Introduction and Notes by Martin S. Dworkin

THE SUPREME COURT AND EDUCATION
Edited by David Fellman

INTERNATIONAL EDUCATION
A Documentary History
Edited by David G. Scanlon

CRUSADE AGAINST IGNORANCE
Thomas Jefferson on Education
Edited by Gordon C. Lee

CHINESE EDUCATION UNDER COMMUNISM
Edited by C. T. Hu

CHARLES W. ELIOT AND POPULAR EDUCATION
Edited by Edward A. Krug

WILLIAM T. HARRIS ON EDUCATION
Edited by Martin S. Dworkin (In press)

THE *EMILE* OF JEAN JACQUES ROUSSEAU
Translated and edited by William Boyd

THE MINOR EDUCATIONAL WRITINGS OF
JEAN JACQUES ROUSSEAU
Translated and edited by William Boyd

PSYCHOLOGY AND THE SCIENCE
OF EDUCATION
Selected Writings of Edward L. Thorndike
Edited by Geraldine M. Joncich

THE NEW-ENGLAND PRIMER
Introduction by Paul Leicester Ford

BENJAMIN FRANKLIN ON EDUCATION
Edited by John Hardin Best

THE COLLEGES AND THE PUBLIC
1787-1862
Edited by Theodore R. Crane

TRADITIONS OF AFRICAN EDUCATION
Edited by David G. Scanlon

NOAH WEBSTER'S
AMERICAN SPELLING BOOK
Introductory essay by Henry Steele Commager

Noah Webster's American Spelling Book

With an Introductory Essay by Henry Steele Commager

☆

CLASSICS IN

No. 17

EDUCATION

☆

BUREAU OF PUBLICATIONS
TEACHERS COLLEGE, COLUMBIA UNIVERSITY
NEW YORK

PREFACE

"Just published," read the unassuming advertisement in the *Connecticut Courant* for October 7, 1783, " 'The First Part of a *Grammatical Institute of the English Language* . . .' by Noah Webster, A.M., 10ˢ per dozen or 14ᵈ per single book." Thereby was Noah Webster's blue-backed speller formally announced to the American public. Messrs. Hudson and Goodwin, publishers of the *Courant,* had reluctantly agreed to print the little volume, but only after the author himself had consented to underwrite the costs. Book publishing, after all, was a risky business, and who could foretell the prospects of a new speller that looked suspiciously like the very volumes it was meant to displace.

The outcome, of course, is one of the fabulous chapters in the history of American publishing. The first printing was exhausted by May of 1784; others followed in rapid succession. In 1807, Webster estimated the annual sale at 200,000 copies; by 1837, he estimated the total sale to date at fifteen million. D. Appleton and Company took over the plates in 1855; and when an interviewer in 1880 inquired of William H. Appleton as to the firm's best-selling book, Appleton replied: "Webster's Speller; and it has the largest sale of any book in the world except the Bible. We sell a million copies a year."

Webster's bibliographers indicate that the facsimile edition of *The American Spelling Book* here presented was the 236th version to appear under that title in the United States. All together, six editions were published as part one of *The Grammatical Institute;* 254 as *The American Spelling Book;* and 128 as *The Elementary Spelling Book.* After 1845 countless other adaptations appeared under a variety of titles.

Those who would inquire further into the history and influence of the speller might profitably consult Emily Ellsworth *et al.: A Bibliography of the Writings of Noah Webster* (New York, 1958); Emily Ellsworth Fowler Ford: *Notes on the Life of Noah Webster* (2 vols., New York, 1912); Horace E. Scudder: *Noah Webster* (Boston, 1881); Ervin C. Shoemaker: *Noah Webster: Pioneer of Learning* (New York, 1936); and Harry R. Warfel: *Noah*

Webster: Schoolmaster to America (New York, 1936). Warfel's volume is the most authoritative biography of Webster to date; Shoemaker's is the most scholarly assessment of his contribution to American education.

LAWRENCE A. CREMIN

"Schoolmaster to America"

By HENRY STEELE COMMAGER

IN 1783 the United States achieved independence, and President Ezra Stiles of Yale College prophesied that the new nation, happily free of those provincial dialects that confused social and regional differences in less fortunate countries, would be bound together by a single and uniform language. At that very time a young graduate of Yale, teaching obscurely in Goshen, New York, proclaimed what was to be a cultural and linguistic Declaration of Independence. Noah Webster wanted to call his little book "The American Instructor," but the dignified President Stiles overruled him and dictated the pretentious title, "A Grammatical Institute of the English Language: Part I." It was in fact nothing more impressive than a Speller; to generations of Americans it was to be familiarly known as "Webster's Blue-Backed Speller." It caught on, at once; within a few years it all but monopolized the field; under its benign guidance generations of young Americans learned the same words, the same spellings, the same pronunciations; read the same stories; absorbed the same moral lessons.

It was all part of a larger program—a program for cultural as well as political independence from the Mother Country. "America," wrote the young pedagogue, "must be independent in literature as she is in politics"; and in the Preface of his Speller he elaborated on this notion:

> The author wishes to promote the honor and prosperity of the confederated republics of America. . . . This country must in some future time be as distinguished by the superiority of her literary improvements, as she is already by the liberality of her civil and ecclesiastical constitutions. Europe is grown old in folly, corruption and tyranny. For

1

> America in her infancy to adopt the maxims of the
> Old World would be to stamp the wrinkles of de-
> crepit old age upon the bloom of youth, and to
> plant the seeds of decay in a vigorous constitution.
> American glory begins to dawn at a favourable
> period. . . .

It was characteristic of Webster that he should associate
the dawn of American glory with the publication of his
own book, and it was prophetic, too, for the connection
was there, and it was soon to be notorious. In 1783 Webster had few qualifications for either education or phi-
lology, but enormous enthusiasm for both. It was a sound
instinct that directed his energies into these fields, and
held them there through a long life of distractions, ambitions, and conceits.

The Speller, and after it the Grammar, the Reader,
and the Dictionaries, assured Webster a place among
the Founding Fathers. Over the years he consolidated his
position, and extended it. Indeed, wherever we look there
is Noah Webster, dour, angular, and aggressive, busily
fathering institutions and organizations that we now think
of as characteristically American. Even in an age of
Fatherhood, he was fabulously progenitive, and insistent,
too, on his parental prerogatives. He was, clearly, the
Father of the American language, and he was certainly
one of the Fathers of American education. If we turn to
that group of statesmen who made the Constitution,
there is Webster, holding aloft his "Sketches of American
Policy," and determined to be numbered among the
Founding Fathers. He presents himself no less insistently
as one of the Fathers of American political thought, for
in voluminous pages he told Hamilton how to run parties, lectured Madison on the Presidency, and instructed
Jefferson on the nature of democracy. If we look to
journalism, there is Webster, editor of the *American*
Magazine, of the *Minerva* and the *Herald*, and all ready
to toss off a history of American journalism.

If we consider science there, too, is Webster, edging
up to Dr. Franklin and Dr. Rush and Dr. Rittenhouse,

hopefully proffering his two-volume "History of Epidemics," and with sheafs of scientific articles bulging in his coat pockets. He is surely the Father of Copyright; he has some claim to be the Father of the Census. What with his school histories, and his edition (or was it his?) of Winthrop's Journal, he is one of the Fathers of American history; and his many essays on banking, finance, and insurance support his claim to be a Father of American Economics as well. And finally his singlehanded revision of the Bible—he thought it his greatest work—permits us to call him one of the Fathers of the Church!

II

EVEN in an age of versatility, it is an astonishing versatility. And yet it does not quite ring true. The versatility of a Franklin, a Jefferson, a Bentley, a Rush, a Rumford is the spontaneous expression of a complex personality and an affluent and extravagant nature. But with Webster versatility seems to be the expression, rather, of nagging ambition, grim determination, and indefatigable officiousness, and perhaps of vanity as well. He was determined to make his mark; he was not going to be left out; and he was confident that whatever he touched he improved.

For all his wide and varied interests, he did not have a richly-stored mind; for all his vitality he did not have an open mind; narrow, cold, almost passionless, he was wholly lacking in those grace-notes his great contemporaries added to their scores with such ease. He read everything, but in order to get definitions for his dictionary; he taught music, but revealed not the slightest interest in the musical giants of his own time; he studied history, but only to learn that man is vile. He knew the languages of twenty nations, but was interested in none of these; he visited France only to deplore its licentiousness; he visited Cambridge, only to remark on the inferiority of its architecture. He was devout, but curiously untouched by religious sentiment. Religion was to him a kind of muscular exercise in moralizing; he was ready to drop his closest friend, Joel Barlow, because he found his poetry godless; and he thought the Bible would be

improved by expunging the word "womb." He was zeal-
ous for education, but had little faith in the young, and
thought voting should be restricted to those over forty-
five. His reason for founding Amherst College was chiefly
to confound and frustrate Unitarian Harvard. He was a
cultural busybody; in an odd fashion he anticipated Big
Bill Thompson's wonderful boast about Chicago: he took
up culture, and he made culture hum.

And yet this is an ungrateful view; it is not what Webster was that is important, but what Webster did. And
what he did is inescapably clear. He helped free generations of Americans from a sense of inferiority about
their language, and gave them instead a sense of the dig-
nity of their speech. He contributed more than any other
single person to a uniform American speech, and to the
avoidance of those differences in accent and vocabulary
that might proclaim differences in background, in class,
or in region. His wish was, he said,

> to diffuse an uniformity and purity of language in
> America, to destroy the provincial prejudices that
> originate in the trifling differences of dialect and
> produce reciprocal ridicule, to promote the interest
> of literature and the harmony of the United States.

More specifically, he labored, in his books and his news-
papers and his teaching,

> to extirpate the improprieties and vulgarisms which
> were necessarily introduced by settlers from various
> parts of Europe; to reform the abuses and cor-
> ruption which tincture the conversation of the
> polite part of Americans; to render the acquisition
> of the language easy both to American youth and
> foreigners; and to render the pronounciation of it
> accurate and uniform by demolishing those odious
> distinctions of provincial dialects which are the
> subject of reciprocal ridicule.

All this Webster achieved, first through that **Speller**

which went triumphantly from generation to generation
until it came to be as familiar as the Bible, and as essential; through the Readers which for a time commanded
the field and yielded only reluctantly to the more popular
Peter Parley and McGuffey series; through his famous
Dictionary which appeared first, and modestly, in 1806,
and then monumentally in 1828 and through all its
metamorphoses achieved the distinction of being an in-
stitution in itself. It was the Speller that conquered the
land. It established its sovereignty in the East; it went
west with the Conestoga wagon, and in the knapsacks
of countless itinerant pedagogues; it leaped the mountains and established its empire on the Pacific coast; it
even invaded the South, and on the eve of that war he
was to do much to bring on Jefferson Davis wrote "above
all other people we are one, and above all books which
have united us in the bond of common language, I
place the good old Spelling-Book of Noah Webster."
The demand was insatiable; it sold by the hundred
thousand, it sold by the million, it sold by the tens of
millions. No other secular book had ever spread so wide,
penetrated so deep, lasted so long.

III

NEITHER energy nor ambition nor vanity explains anything by itself, for we want to know why these forces
took one channel rather than another: why they contributed to social weal rather than woe; found outlet in
public rather than in private activities; expressed themselves in national rather than parochial accents, in
liberal rather than conservative terms. The driving force
in Webster, the compulsion that explains all particular
expressions of his ambitions and his energies, was nationalism.

It was, to be sure, an age of self-conscious nationalism,
and Webster was typical rather than original. "We are
laboring hard to establish in this country principles more
and more national, and free from all foreign ingredients,"
wrote Alexander Hamilton. We must have an American
literature, argued Joel Barlow and Philip Freneau and

Timothy Dwight. "The business of education acquired a new complexion by the independence of our country," said Benjamin Rush. "One American work is of more value to the United States than three foreign ones, even of superior merit," wrote Horatio Greenough of painting. "The Churches of America are all assuming a new complexion," wrote Dr. John Livingston; "they now become National Churches in this new Empire." Even arithmetic was to be new, for, "as the United States are now an independent nation," said Nicholas Pike, "it was judged that a system might be calculated more suitable to our Meridian than those heretofore published." This was the climate of opinion in which Webster lived and flourished; this was the doctrine to which he enthusiastically subscribed, the gospel he gladly preached. "Unshackle your minds," he admonished his countrymen. "You have an empire to raise and support by your exertions, and a national character to establish and extend by your wisdom and virtue. Every engine," he added, "should be employed to render the people of this country national, to call their attachments home to their own country, and to inspire them with the pride of national character."

The nations of the Old World were the products of centuries of history; America was created. Old World nations had inherited and absorbed all the essential ingredients of nationalism; America had to manufacture them. The peoples of other countries had been born national, as had their fathers and their forebears; in America they were to be "rendered" national. What were the "engines" to be employed in this enterprise?

One of them, and one of the most important, was language. "A national language," Webster said, "is a bond of national union." And so it was—in France, in Denmark, in England, in Spain; and when ancient peoples organized themselves as independent nations in Germany, in Italy, in Greece, in Bohemia. The new United States was fortunate in having a common (even if an inherited) language; could that language be kept common over an immense territory, and among a people made up of so many and such diverse elements? The question might seem more pertinent to the twentieth than to the early nineteenth century; that it is not, is because Webster and his colleagues not only asked it but answered it over a century ago.

The peoples of Old World nations had, indeed, their own language, but their language was neither common nor uniform. Everywhere on the Continent the upper-classes spoke French, and disdained the vernacular. Each region had its own dialect and each class its own idiom. So pronounced were the local dialects that Frenchmen from Brittany and the Languedoc could not understand each other, or Germans from the Rhineland and Saxony, or Danes from Copenhagen and Jutland, or, for that matter, Englishmen from East Anglia and Devonshire. And if, almost everywhere, speech proclaimed region, it betrayed class, and continued to do so down into our own century; just a few years ago George Orwell could say that every Englishman was branded on the tongue at birth. In the Old World these linguistic vagaries were not seriously divisive (not yet, anyhow) because the classes who confessed them had little influence and because there were so many other forces—religion, for example, or history, or the Monarchy—binding men together.

But if nationalism was to work in the United States—and in 1800 that was still very much an open question—it would have to get along without the Monarchy, the Church, the Military, and the many other institutions that provided common denominators abroad, and work with more democratic ingredients and build on more popular support. It would have to frustrate those class and religious and racial divisions which were potentially so dangerous; it would have to overcome differences not merely of accent but of language itself. The United States, dedicated to the unprecedented experiment of republicanism in a vast territory, a heterogeneous population, and a classless society, could not afford differences of accent or of language.

A great many Americans of the eighteenth century saw this, but none more clearly than Webster. He labored not only for a common language, but for an *American* language. Like Franklin and Jefferson he rejected the authority of the hated Dr. Johnson, and of Dr. Robert Lowth as well; indeed, he rejected all English authority that seemed to conflict with common sense or common usage. He knew that language was a living thing, and was confident that Americans had the same capacity to enlarge it and adapt it as the English, and that their contribution was not only respectable but desirable. "New circumstances," he said, "new modes of life, new laws, new ideas of various kinds" would bring about "considerable differences between the American and the English language." Those differences would be, for the most part, improvements, for "the English language has been greatly improved in Britain within a century, but its highest perfection with every other branch of human knowledge is perhaps reserved for the land of light and freedom." With what was in his day considerable boldness Webster admitted to his spellers and readers, and eventually to his dictionaries, words regarded in the Mother Country as obsolete or as barbarisms. He accepted new grammatical constructions. He adopted a simplified spelling—much more simplified, indeed, than public opinion would stand, then or later. And he defined words in American rather than in English terms: this was one of his most significant contributions. In all of this he found authority in popular usage.

IV

For how was the uniformity of the American language to be achieved? Could it be imposed from above? So John Adams thought, and he had early recommended the creation of an American Academy which should fix the standards of good usage. Webster himself was instrumental in establishing a Philological Society whose chief function seems to have been to endorse his own books; certainly it did nothing else memorable. The Academy was never born; the Society withered and died; but they were not necessary. Webster's books did their work. He found his authority in part in what he thought the less corrupt

usage of Elizabethan England, but more clearly in popular (mostly New England) usage. "The *general practice*
of a nation is the rule of propriety," he wrote, "and this
practice should at least be consulted in so important a
matter, as that of making laws for speaking." It was the
"general practice" that he tried to incorporate in his
spellers, grammars, readers, and dictionaries, but these,
in turn, became authorities. They were, however, authorities with a difference—authorities that (like our governments) drew their power from below, and that were em-
braced, spontaneously, by the people themselves. Webster
was therefore not only a standard and a symbol, but a
spontaneous standard and a popular symbol. When, in
1830, he went to Washington to push through a new
(and more profitable) copyright law, he was welcomed
with reverence by Congressmen, almost all of whom had
been brought up on his books.

A nation needs not only a common language; it needs,
even more, a common past, and a sense of that past.
Every European statemaker of modern times has recognized this. Thus, Bishop Grundtvig in Denmark devoted
his volcanic energies to the editing of ancient Danish
ballads, the writing of national histories and national
songs, the resurrection of the national past. Thus, in
Germany Schlegel and Stein and Savigny and the
brothers Grimm recreated the German past in order to
create a German future. Thus, in his struggle for the
unification of Italy Mazzini was always conscious that
"the most important inspiration for nationalism is the
awareness of past glories and past sufferings." The phi-
losophers and historians of nationalism, too, recognized
the primacy of tradition. Thus, Ernst Renan emphasized
for France "the common memories, glories, afflictions,
and regrets"; thus, in England John Stuart Mill concluded that the most important single ingredient in nationalism was "the possession of a national history and
community of recollections." And our contemporary,
Sir Ernest Barker, has put the matter succinctly: "A
nation is not the physical fact of one blood but the
mental fact of one tradition."

All true enough, but what was the new United States
to do? How does a country without a past—without, in
any event, a common past—provide itself with a usable
past, or with a substitute for it? How does a country without history, traditions, legends, or symbols create them?
And how does it find substitutes for those institutions
and symbols which customarily served to unify Old
World peoples: the Monarchy, the Aristocracy, the
Church, the Army, the University, and others?

V

YET all the American past lacked was antiquity, and
antiquity, like tradition, could be manufactured. Americans were perhaps the first people to prove what so many
of the newer peoples of the twentieth century are now
proving, that the past can be telescoped, and the proc-
esses of tradition-making and symbol-making enormously
accelerated. Undaunted by their youth, Americans set
about resolutely to create what was missing; with immense energy they provided themselves with a common
history, a common memory, a set of symbols and of
legends. Almost everyone joined in this enterprise:
statesmen, soldiers, poets, historians, journalists, ex-
plorers, artists, scholars, and teachers.

Webster, it will be noted, fitted into most of these
categories, but particularly the last one. It was characteristic—it was almost prophetic—that in America the
teacher should play a larger role in the creation of nationalism than almost anywhere else: this because the
United States was the first nation to inaugurate anything
remotely like universal free education. In other countries
governments deliberately used the schools to indoctrinate
the young with particular versions of nationalism and
patriotism. In the United States, government never performed this dangerous role, but private individuals did,
for the most part quite innocently. Noah Webster was
perhaps the first to realize the limitless potentialities of
education for the encouragement of nationalism, and of
the schoolbook as the vehicle. He purposed, from the beginning, to use the schools as engines of nationalism.

That purpose he carried out most fully in his Readers, and, eventually, in a bewildering miscellany of histories of one kind or another: the historical introduction he provided to Jedediah Morse's immensely popular Geography; the "Elements of Useful Knowledge"—one volume devoted to American history; the "Federal Catechism" attached to his "Little Reader's Assistant," and others.

Webster was first in the field with moral and patriotic readers, and set the style for subsequent ventures, notably those of the McGuffey brothers. His Reader (elaborately called An American Selection of Lessons in Reading and Speaking: Calculated to Improve the minds and refine the taste of Youth) was Part III of the Grammatical Institute, but came to have an independent life of its own. From the beginning its purpose was patriotic as well as educational—in Webster's mind these things were never separate. On the title-page Webster placed the absurd admonition by Mirabeau: "Begin with the infant in his cradle; let the first word he lisps be Washington." Later Webster was to rephrase this pious injunction with more elaborate humorlessness: "Every child in America should be acquainted with his own country. As soon as he opens his lips he should rehearse the history of his own country, he should lisp the praise of liberty, and of those illustrious heroes and statesmen who have wrought a revolution in her favor." The Reader included addresses by Warren and Hancock on the Boston massacre; the Declaration of Independence; Washington's Farewell to his army and his Circular Letter to the States; poems from the practised hands of Barlow, Trumbull, and Freneau; and an extract—later withdrawn—from Tom Paine. The filiopietistic purpose was clear, but Webster drove it home: "In the choice of these pieces, I have not been inattentive to the political interests of America. Several of these masterly addresses of Congress . . . contain such *noble, just, and independent sentiments* that I cannot help wishing to transfuse them into the breasts of the rising generation."

Even the Dictionary was exploited for patriotic purposes. It was an *American* dictionary, and its American character was less ostentatious in spelling and grammar and vocabulary than in definitions and illustrations. "The chief glory of a nation," wrote Webster, "is its authors," and it was "with pride and satisfaction" that he cited Washington and Franklin, Adams and Kent, Barlow and Irving, along with Bacon and Milton, Addison and Pope. "I may go further," he boasted somewhat indiscriminately, "and affirm that our country has produced some of the best models of composition . . . President Smith (of Princeton); the authors of the Federalist; Chancellor Kent; the prose of Mr. Barlow, and of Dr. William Channing, of Washington Irving . . . in purity, in elegance, and in technical precision, is equalled only by that of the best British authors, and surpassed by that of no English compositions of a similar kind."

Webster's patriotism, to be sure, was ardent but particular. In the beginning broad and generous, embracing the whole of the Union, and all classes of society, it grew increasingly narrow and sectional and ungenerous. He had begun as a disciple of Franklin, an admirer of Jefferson; he ended as an honorary member of the Essex Junto and a crony to the despicable Timothy Pickering. He had begun as a champion of nationalism, republicanism, and democracy; the French Revolution persuaded him to abjure democracy; Jefferson inspired doubts about republicanism; and the Hartford Convention was—for a time at least—the measure of his political nationalism. However, if he never became reconciled to democracy, he did become reconciled to the new form nationalism assumed after 1812.

But we must not expect consistency, or demand it. Webster was, for all his devotion to learning, a creature not of reason but of sentiment. "The eyes of the world are upon me," he wrote hopefully in 1788. We no longer see him, but we speak him and hear him. Surely that is an immortality even beyond his imagining.

THE

AMERICAN

SPELLING BOOK,

CONTAINING

THE RUDIMENTS

OF THE

ENGLISH LANGUAGE

FOR

THE USE OF SCHOOLS

IN THE

UNITED STATES.

BY NOAH WEBSTER, ESQ.

THE REVISED IMPRESSION, WITH THE LATEST CORRECTIONS.

MIDDLETOWN, CONN.
PUBLISHED BY WILLIAM H. NILES.
1831.

PREFACE.

The American Spelling Book, or first Part of a Grammatical Institute of the English language, when first published, encountered an opposition, which few new publications have sustained with success. It, however, maintained its ground, and its reputation has been gradually extended and established, until it has become the principal elementary book in the United States. In a great part of the northern States, it is the only book of the kind used ; it is much used in the middle and southern States ; and its annual sales indicate a large and increasing demand. Its merit is evinced not only by this general use, but by a remarkable fact, that in many attempts made to rival it, the compilers have all constructed their works on a similar plan ; some of them have most unwarrantably and illegally copied a considerable part of the tables, with little or no alteration, and others have altered them, by additions, mutilations and subdivisions, numerous and perplexing. In most instances, this species of injustice has been discountenanced by the citizens of the United States, and the public sentiment has protected the original work more effectually than the penalties of the law.*

---

* The sales of the *American Spelling Book*, since its first publication, amount to more than FIVE MILLIONS of copies, and they are annually increasing. One great advantage experienced in using this work, is the simplicity of the scheme of pronunciation, which exhibits the sounds of the letters with sufficient accuracy, without a mark over each vowel. The multitude of characters in Perry's scheme renders it far too complex and perplexing to be useful to children, confusing the eye without enlightening the understanding. Nor is there the least necessity for a figure over each vowel, as in Walker, Sheridan, and other authors. In nine-tenths of the words in our language, a correct pronunciation is better taught by a natural division of the syllables, and a direction for placing the accent, than by a minute and endless repetition of characters. *March,* 1818.

PREFACE.

Gratitude to the public, as well as a desire to furnish schools with a more complete and well digested system of elements, has induced me to embrace the opportunity when the first patent expires, to revise the work, and give it all the improvement which the experience of many teachers, and my own observations and reflections have suggested. In the execution of this design, care has been taken to preserve the scheme of pronunciation, and the substance of the former work. Most of the tables, having stood the test of experience, are considered as susceptible of little improvement or amendment. A few alterations are made, with a view to accommodate the work to the most accurate rules of pronunciation, and most general usage of speaking ; as also to correct some errors which had crept into the work. A perfect standard of pronunciation, in a living language, is not to be expected ; and when the best English dictionaries differ from each other, in several hundred, probably a thousand words, where are we to seek for undisputed rules ? and how can we arrive at perfect uniformity ?

The rules respecting accent, prefixed to the former work, are found to be too lengthy and complex, to answer any valuable purpose in a work intended for children ; they are therefore omitted. The geographical tables are thrown into a different form ; and the abridgment of grammar is omitted. Geography and Grammar are sciences that require distinct treatises, and schools are furnished with them in abundance. It is believed to be more useful to confine this work to its proper objects, the teaching of the first elements of the language, spelling and reading. On this subject, the opinion of many judicious persons concurs with my own.

The improvements made in this work, chiefly consist in a great number of new tables. Some of them are intended to exhibit the manner in which derivative words, and the variations of nouns, adjectives, and verbs, are formed. The examples of this sort cannot fail to be very useful ; as children, who may be well acquainted with a word in the singular number, or positive degree, may be perplex-

PREFACE.

ed when they see it in the plural number, or comparative form. The examples of derivation, will accustom youth to observe the manner in which various branches spring from one radical word, and thus lead their minds to some knowledge of the formation of the language, and the manner in which syllables are added or prefixed to vary the sense of words.

In the familiar lessons for reading, care has been taken to express ideas in plain, but not in vulgar language; and to combine, with the familiarity of objects, useful truth, and practical principles.

In a copious list of names of places, rivers, lakes, mountains, &c. which are introduced into this work, no labor has been spared to exhibit their just orthography and pronunciation, according to the analogies of our language, and the common usages of the country. The orthography of Indian names has not, in every instance, been well adjusted by American authors. Many of these names still retain the French orthography, found in the writings of the first discoverers or early travellers; but the practice of writing such words in the French manner ought to be discountenanced. How does an unlettered American know the pronunciation of the names, *Ouisconsin* or *Ouabasche*, in this French dress? Would he suspect the pronunciation to be Wisconsin and Waubash? Our citizens ought not to be thus perplexed with an orthography to which they are strangers. Nor ought the harsh guttural sounds of the natives to be retained in such words as Shawangunk, and many others. Where popular practice has softened and abridged words of this kind, the change has been made in conformity to the genius of our language, which is accommodated to a civilized people; and the orthography ought to be conformed to the practice of speaking. The true pronunciation of the name of a place, is that which prevails in and near the place. I have always sought for this, but am apprehensive that, in some instances, my information may not

PREFACE.

be correct. It has however been my endeavor to give the true pronunciation, in the appropriate English characters.

The importance of correctness and uniformity in the several impressions of a book of such general use, has suggested the propriety of adopting effectual measures to insure these desirable objects; and it is believed that such measures are taken, as will render all the future impressions of this work, uniform in the pages, well executed, and perfectly correct.

In the progress of society and improvement, some gradual changes must be expected in a living language, and corresponding alterations in elementary books of instruction become indispensable: but it is desirable that these alterations should be as few as possible, for they occasion uncertainty and inconvenience. And although perfect uniformity in speaking is not probably attainable in any living language, yet it is to be wished that the youth of our country may be, as little as possible, perplexed with various differing systems and standards. Whatever may be the difference of opinion among individuals respecting a few particular words, or the particular arrangement of a few classes of words, the general interest of education requires that a disposition to multiply books and systems for teaching the language of the country, should not be indulged to an unlimited extent. On this disposition, however, the public sentiment alone can impose restraint.

As the first part of the Institute met with the general approbation of my fellow citizens, it is presumed the labor bestowed upon this work, in correcting and improving the system, will render it still more acceptable to the public, by facilitating the education of youth, and enabling teachers to instil into their minds, with the first rudiments of the language, some just ideas of religion, morals and domestic economy.   N. W.

New-Haven, 1803.

ANALYSIS OF SOUNDS

IN THE

ENGLISH LANGUAGE.

LANGUAGE, in its more limited sense, is the expression of ideas by articulate sounds. In a more general sense, the word denotes all sounds by which animals express their feelings, in such a manner as to be understood by their own species.

Articulate sounds are those which are formed by the human voice, in pronouncing letters, syllables and words, and constitute the *spoken* language which is addressed to the *ear*. Letters are the marks of sounds, and the first elements of *written* language, which is presented to the *eye*.

In a perfect language, every simple sound would be expressed by a distinct character; and no character would have more than one sound. But languages are not thus perfect; and the English Language, in particular, is, in these respects, extremely irregular.

The letters used in writing, when arranged in a certain customary order, compose what is called an *Alphabet*.

The English Alphabet consists of twenty-six letters, or single characters; and for want of others, certain simple sounds are represented by two letters united.

The letters or single characters are, a, b, c, d, e, f, g, h, i, j, k, l, m, n, o, p, q, r, s, t, u, v, w, x, y, z. The compound characters, representing distinct sounds, are, ch, sh, th. There is also a distinct sound expressed by *ng*, as in *long;* and another by *s* or *z*, as in *fusion, azure,* which sound might be represented by *zh*.

Letters are of two kinds, *vowels* and *consonants*.

A vowel is a simple, articulate sound, formed without the help of another letter, by opening the mouth in a particular manner, and begun and completed with the same position of the organs, as *a, e, o*. The letters which represent these sounds are six; *a, e, i, o, u, y*. But each of these characters is used to express two or more sounds.

An Easy Standard of Pronunciation.

The following are the vowel sounds in the English Language—of *a*, as in late, ask, ball, hat, what.

of *e*, in mete, met.

of *i*, in find, pit.

of *o*, in note, not, move.

of *u*, in truth, but, bush.

of *y*, in chyle, pity.

The vowels have a long and a short sound, or quantity; and the different quantities are represented by different letters. Thus.

Long	*a*, in late,	when shortened, is expressed	by *e*, as in let.
	ee, in feet,		by *i*, in fit, & *y*, in pity.
	oo, in pool,		by *u*, in pull, & *oo* in wool.
	a, in hall,		by *o*, in holly, & *a*, in wallow.

That the sounds of *a* in *late*, and *e* in *iet*, are only a modification of the same vowel, may be easily understood by attending to the manner of forming the sounds; for in both words, the aperture of the mouth and the configuration of the organs are the same. This circumstance proves the sameness of the sound or vowel, in the two words, though differing in time or quantity.

A consonant is a letter which has no sound, or an imperfect one, without the help of a vowel. The consonants which are entirely silent, interrupt the voice by closing the organs; as b, d, g hard, k, p, t, which are called *mutes*; as in eb, ed, eg, ek, ep, et.

The consonants which do not entirely interrupt all sound by closing the organs, are f, l, m, n, r, s, v, z, which are all half vowels, or semi-vowels. To these may be added the sounds of sh, th, zh, and ng, in esh, eth, ezh, ing, which our language has no single characters to express.

A diphthong is the union of two simple sounds uttered in one breath or articulation. The two sounds do not strictly form one; for there are two different positions of

An Easy Standard of Pronunciation.

of the organs, and two distinct sounds; but the transition from one to the other is so rapid that the distinction is scarcely perceived, and the sound is therefore considered as compound. Dipthongal sounds are sometimes represented by two letters, as in *voice*, *joy*, and sometimes by one, as in *defy;* the sound of *y*, in the latter word, if prolonged, terminates in *e*, and is really dipthongal.

A tripthong is the union of three vowels in a syllable; but it may be questioned whether in any English word, we pronounce three vowels in a single articulation. In the word *adieu*, the three vowels are not distinctly sounded.

B has but one sound, as in bite.

C is always sounded like *k* or *s*—like *k*, before *a*, *o*, and *u*—and like *s* before *e*, *i*, and *y*. Thus,

ca, ce, ci, co, cu, cy,
ka, se, si, ko, ku, sy.

At the end of words it is always hard like *k*, as in *public*. When followed by *i* or *e* before a vowel, the syllable slides into the sound of *sh*, as in cetaceous, gracious, social, which are pronounced cetashus, grashus, soshal.

D has only one sound, as in dress, bold.

F has its own proper sound, as in life, fever, except in *of*, where it has the sound of *v*.

G before *a*, *o*, and *u*, has always its hard sound, as in gave, go, gun.

Before *e*, *i*, and *y*, it has the same hard sound in some words, and in others the sound of *j*. But these varieties are incapable of being reduced to any general rule, and are to be learnt only by practice, observation, and a dictionary, in which the sounds are designated.

H can hardly be said to have any sound, but it denotes an aspiration or impulse of breath, which modifies the sound of the following vowel, as in heart, heave.

I is a vowel, as in fit; or a consonant, as in bullion.

J is the mark of a compound sound, or union of sounds, which may be represented by *dzh*, or the soft *g*, as in jelly.

An Easy Standard of Pronunciation.

K has but one sound, as in king ; and before *n* is always silent, as in know.

L has but one sound, as in lame.   It is silent before *k*, as in walk.

M has but one sound, as in man ; and is never silent.

N has but one sound, as in not ; and is silent after *m*, as in hymn.

P has one uniform sound, as in pit.

Q has the power of *k*, and is always followed by *u*, as in question.

R has one sound only, as in barrel.

S has the sound of *c* as in *so ;* of *z*, as in rose—and when followed by *i* preceding a vowel, the syllable has the sound of *sh*, as in mission ; or *zh*, as in osier.

T has its proper sound, as in *turn*, at the beginning of words and end of syllables.   In all terminations in *tion*, and *tial*, *ti* have the sound of *sh*, as in nation, nuptial ; except when preceded by *s* or *x*, in which cases they have the sound of *ch*, as in question, mixtion.

U has the properties of a consonant and vowel, in union, unanimity, &c.

V has uniformly one sound, as in voice, live, and is never silent.

W has the power of a vowel, as in dwell ; or a consonant, as in well, will.

X has the sound of *ks*, as in wax ; or of *gz*, as in exist, and in other words, when followed by an accented syllable beginning with a vowel.   In the beginning of Greek names, it has the sound of *z*, as in Xerxes, Xenophon.

Y is a vowel, as in vanity ; a dipthong, as in defy ; or a consonant, as in young.

Z has its own sound usually, as in zeal, freeze.

Ch have the sound of *tsh* in words of English origin, as in chip—in some words of French original, they have the sound of *sh*, as in machine—and in some words of Greek origin, the sound of *k*, as in chorus.

Gh have the sound of *f*, as in laugh ; or are silent, as in light.

An Easy Standard of Pronunciation.

Ph have the sound of *f*, as in philosophy ; except in Stephen, where the sound is that of *v*.

Ng have a nasal sound, as in sing ; but when *e* follows *g*, the latter takes the sound of *j*, as in range. In the words, longer, stronger, younger, the sound of the *g* is doubled, and the last syllable is sounded as if written long-ger, &c.

Sh has one sound only, as in shell ; but its use is often supplied by *ti*, *ci*, and *ce*, before a vowel, as in motion, gracious, cetaceous.

Th has two sounds, aspirate and vocal—aspirate, as in think, bath—vocal, as in those, that, bathe.

Sc before *a*, *o*, *u* and *r*, are pronounced like *sk*, as in scale, scoff, sculpture, scribble : before *e*, *i*, *y*, like soft *c*, or *s*, as in scene, sceptic, science, scythian. Thus pronounced,

sca, sce, sci, sco, scu, scy,
ska, se, si, sko, sku, sy.

Formation of Words and Sentences.

Letters form syllables, syllables form words, and words form sentences, which compose a discourse.

A syllable is a letter, or a union of letters, which can be uttered at one impulse of voice.

A word of one syllable is called a monosyllable.

of two syllables   a dissyllable.
of three syllables   a trissyllable.
of many syllables   a polysyllable.

Of Accent, Emphasis, and Cadence.

Accent is a forcible stress or impulse of voice on a letter or syllable, distinguishing it from others in the same word. When it falls on a vowel, it prolongs the sound, as in glory ; when it falls on a consonant, the preceding vowel is short, as in habit.

The general rule by which accent is regulated, is, that the stress of voice falls on that syllable of a word which

An Easy Standard of Pronunciation.

renders the articulation most easy to the speaker, and most agreeable to the hearer. By this rule has the accent of most words been imperceptibly established by long and universal consent.

When a word consists of three or more syllables, the ease of speaking requires usually a secondary accent, of less forcible utterance than the primary, but clearly distinguishable from the pronunciation of unaccented syllables: as superfluity, literary.

In many compound words, the parts of which are important words of themselves, there is very little distinction of accent; as ink-stand, church-yard.

Emphasis is a particular force of utterance given to a particular word in a sentence, on account of its importance.

Cadence is a fall or modulation of the voice in reading or speaking, especially at the end of a sentence.

Words are simple or compound, primitive or derivative.

A simple word cannot be divided, without destroying the sense; as man, child, house, charity, faith.

A compound word is formed by two or more words; as chimney-piece, book-binder.

Primitive words are such as are not derived, but constitute a radical stock from which others are formed; as grace, hope, charm.

Derivative words are those which are formed of a primitive, and some termination or additional syllable; as grace-less, hope-ful, charm-ing, un-welcome.

Spelling is the art or practice of writing or reading the proper letters of a word, called also orthography. In forming tables for learners, the best rule to be observed, is, to divide the syllables in such a manner as to guide the learner by the sound of the letters, to the sound of the words; that is, to divide them as they are divided in a just pronunciation.

An Easy Standard of Pronunciation.

Key to the following Work.

Long.			*Short ab.*		
1	1	1	5	5	5
a	name,	late.	a	what,	was.
e *or* ee	here,	feet.	o	not,	from.
i	time,	find.		*Oo proper.*	
o	note,	fort.	6	6	6
u *or* ew	tune,	new.	o *or* oo	move,	room.
y	dry,	defy.		*Oo short.*	
			7	7	7
	Short.		oo	book,	stood.
2	2	2	u	bush,	full.
a	man,	hat.		*Short u.*	
e	men,	let.	8	8	8
i	pit,	pin.	i	sir,	bird.
u	tun,	but.	o	come,	love.
y	glory,	Egypt.	e	her.	
				Long a.	
	Broad a or *aw.*		9	9	9
3	3	3	e	there,	vein.
a	bald,	tall.		*Long e.*	
o	cost,	sought.	10	10	10
aw	law.		i	fatigue,	pique.
			oi		
	Flat a.		oy	} dipthong ; voice, joy.	
4	4	4	ou		
a	ask,	part.	ow	} dipthong ; loud, now.	

Explanation of the Key.

A figure stands as the invariable representative of a certain sound. The figure 1 represents the long sound of the letters, *a, e, i, o, u,* or *ew,* and *y;* number 2, the short sound of the same characters: number 3, marks the sound of ·broad *a,* as in *hall :* number 4 represents the sound of *a,* in *father :* number 5, represents the short sound of broad *a,* as in *not, what :* number 6 represents the sound of *o* in *move,* commonly expressed by *oo :* number 7, represents the short sound of *oo* in *root,*

An Easy Standard of Pronunciation.

bush : number 8 represents the sound of *u* short, made by *e, i,* and *o,* as in *her, bird, come,* pronounced *kur, burd, cum :* number 9 represents the first sound of *a* made by *e,* as in *their, vein,* pronounced *thare, vane :* number 10 represents the French sound of *i,* which is the same as *e* long.

The sounds of the dipthongs *oi* and *ou* are not represented by figures ; these have one invariable sound, and are placed before the words where they occur in the tables.

Silent letters are printed in Italic characters. Thus in he*a*d, g*o*al, b*u*ild, pe*o*ple, fi*g*ht, the Italic letters have no sound.

S, when printed in Italic, is not silent, but pronounced like *z,* as in *devise,* pronounced *devize.*

The letter *e* at the end of words of more syllables than one, is almost always silent ; but serves often to lengthen a foregoing vowel, as in *bid, bide :* to soften *c,* as in *notice :* or to soften *g,* as in *homage :* or to change the sound of *th* from the first to the second, as in *bath, bathe.* In the following work, when *e* final lengthens the foregoing vowel, that is, gives it its first sound, it is printed in a Roman character, as in *fate :* but in all other cases it is printed in Italic, except in table 39.

Ch have the English sound, as in *charm :* except in the 38th and 39th tables.

The sounds of *th* in *this* and *thou,* are all distinguished in the 12th and 37th tables ; except in numeral adjectives.

The sound of *aw* is invariably that of broad *a,* and that of *ew* nearly the same as *u* long.

N. B. Although one character is sufficient to express a simple sound, yet the combinations *ee, aw, ew, oo,* are so well known to express certain sounds, that it was judged best to print both letters in Roman characters. *Ck* and *ss* are also printed in Roman characters, though one alone would be sufficient to express the sound.

An Easy Standard of Pronunciation.

THE ALPHABET

Roman Letters.	Italic.	Names of Letters.
a A	*a A*	a
b B	*b B*	be
c C	*c C*	ce
d D	*d D*	de
e E	*e E*	e
f F	*f F*	ef
g G	*g G*	je
h H	*h H*	he, *or* aytch
i I	*i I*	i
j J	*j J*	ja
k K	*k K*	ka
l L	*l L*	el
m M	*m M*	em
n N	*n N*	en
o O	*o O*	o
p P	*p P*	pe
q Q	*q Q*	cu
r R	*r R*	er
s S	*s S*	es
t T	*t T*	te
u U	*u U*	u
v V	*v V*	ve
w W	*w W*	oo
x X	*x X*	eks
y Y	*y Y*	wi, *or* ye
z Z	*z Z*	ze
&*	*&.*	and

Double Letters.

ff, ffl, fi, fl, ffi.

* This is not a letter, but a character standing for *and*. Children should therefore be taught to call it *and*, not *and per se*.

An Easy Standard of Pronunciation.

TABLE I.

LESSON I.						LESSON VI.				
ba	be	bi	bo	bu	by	ak	ek	ik	ok	uk
ca	ce*	ci*	co	cu˙	cy*	at	et	it	ot	ut
da	de	di	do	du	dy	ar	er	ir	or	ur
fa	fe	fi	'fo	fu	fy	az	ez	iz	oz	uz
ka	ke	ki	ko	ku	ky					

LESSON II.						LESSON VII.				
ga	ge	gi	go	gu	gy	b a	ble	bli	blo	blu
ha	he	hi	ho	hu	hy	cla	cle	cli	clo	clu
ma	me	mi	mo	mu	my	pla	ple	pli	plo	plu
na	ne	ni	no	nu	ny	fla	fle	fli	flo	flu
ra	re	ri	ro	ru	ry	va	ve	vi	vo	vu
ta	te	ti	to	tu	ty					
wa	we	wi	wo	wu	wy					

LESSON III.						LESSON VIII.				
la	le	li	lo	lu	ly	bra	bre	bri	bro	bru
pa	pe	pi	po	pu	py	cra	cre	cri	cro	cru
sa	se	si	so	su	sy	pra	pre	pri	pro	pru
za	ze	zi	zo	zu	zy	gra	gre	gri	gro	gru
						pha	phe	phi	pho	phu

LESSON IV.						LESSON IX.				
ab	eb	ib	ob	ub		cha	che	chi	cho	chu	chy
ac	ec	ic	oc	uc		dra	dre	dri	dro	dru˙	dry
ad	ed	id	od	ud		fra	fre	fri	fro	fru	fry
af	ef	if	of	uf		gla	gle	gli	glo	glu	gly
al	el	il	ol	ul							

LESSON V.						LESSON X.				
ag	eg	ig	og	ug		sla	sle	sli	slo	slu	sly
am	em	im	om	um		qua	que	qui	quo		
an	en	in	on	un		sha	she	shi	sho	shu	shy
ap	ep	ip	op	up		spa	spe	spi	spo	spu	spy
as	es	is	os	us							
av	ev	iv	ov	uv		LESSON XI.					
ax	ex	ix	ox	ux		sta	ste	sti	sto	stu	sty
						sca	sce	sci	sco	scu	scy
						tha	the	thi	tho	thu	thy
						tra	tre	tri	tro	tru	try

* They should be taught to pronounce *ce. ci, cy,* like *se, si, sy.*

An Easy Standard of Pronunciation.

LESSON XII.

spla	sple	spli	splo	splu	sply
spra	spre	spri	spro	spru	spry
stra	stre	stri	stro	stru	stry
swa	swe	swi	swo	swu	swy

TABLE II.

Words of one syllable.

Note. A figure placed over the first word, marks the sound of the vowel in all that follow in that column, until contradicted by another figure.

LESSON I.

Bag	big	bog	bug	den	cap	bit	dot
fag	dig	dog	dug	hen	gap	cit	got
cag	fig	fog	hug	men	lap	hit	hot
gag	gig	hog	lug	pen	map	pit	jot
hag	pig	jog	mug	ten	rap	sit	lot
rag	wig	log	tug	wen	tap	wit	not

LESSON II.

Man	fob	bad	bed	bid	fop	het	but
can	job	had	fed	did	hop	get	cut
pan	mob	lad	led	lid	lop	let	but
ran	rob	mad	red	hid	mop	met	nut
van	sob	sad	wed	rid	top	yet	put

LESSON III.

Belt	gilt	band	bled	brag	clod	brad
melt	hilt	hand	bred	drag	plod	clad
felt	milt	land	fled	flag	shod	glad
pelt	jilt	sand	shed	stag	trod	shad

LESSON IV.

Clog	glut	blab	chab	damp	bump	bend
flog	shut	drab	club	camp	jump	lend
frog	smut	crab	drub	lamp	lump	mend
grog	slut	scab	grub	vamp	pump	send

An Easy Standard of Pronunciation.

LESSON V.

Bind	bold	call	bill	bent	best	brim
find	hold	fall	fill	dent	lest	grim
mind	fold	gall	hill	lent	nest	skim
kind	sold	hall	kill	sent	jest	swim
wind	gold	tall	mill	went	pest	trim

LESSON VI.

Lace	dice	fade	bide	cage	bake	dine
mace	mice	lade	ride	page	cake	fine
trace	nice	made	side	rage	make	pine
pace	rice	wade	wide	wage	wake	wine

LESSON VII.

Gale	cape	pipe	cope	dire	date	drive
pale	rape	ripe	hope	hire	hate	five
sale	tape	wipe	rope	fire	fate	hive
vale	ape	type	pope	wire	grate	rive

LESSON VIII.

Dote	file	dame	fare	bore	bone	nose
mote	bile	fame	mare	fore	cone	dose
note	pile	came	rare	tore	hone	hose
vote	vile	name	tare	wore	tone	rose

TABLE III.

LESSON I.

Blank	blush	fleet	brace	price	brine
flank	flush	sheet	chace	slice	shine
frank	plush	street	grace	spice	swine
prank	crush	greet	space	twice	twine

LESSON II.

Band	bless	crime	broke	blade	blame
grand	dress	chime	choke	spade	flame
stand	press	prime	cloke	trade	shame
strand	stress	slime	smoke	shade	frame

An Easy Standard of Pronunciation.

Lesson III.

¹	¹	¹	²	²	²
Brake	glare	brave	hence	mince	bleed
drake	share	crave	fence	since	breed
flake	snare	grave	pence	prince	speed
spake	spare	slave	sense	rinse	steed

Lesson IV.

²	²	¹	²	²	²	¹	¹
And	ill	age	his	rich	less	duke	life
act	ink	aim	has	held	mess	mule	wife
apt	fact	aid	hast	gift	kiss	rule	safe
ell	fan	ice	hath	dull	miss	time	male
ebb	left	ale	add	till	tush	tune	save
egg	self	ace	elf	will	hush	mute	here
end	else	apu	pen	well	desk	maze	robe

Lesson V.

¹	¹	²	²	²	²
Glade	snake	tract	clank	clamp	black
grade	glaze	pact	crank	champ	crack
shave	craze	plant	shank	cramp	match
wave	prate	sang	plank	spasm	patch
quake	slate	fang	clump	splash	fetch
stage	shape	rang	thump	crash	vetch

Lesson VI.

¹	¹	¹	¹	²	¹
Mine	sire	strife	bride	brick	strive
spine	quire	fife	chide	kick	spike
vine	spire	trite	glide	chick	splice
gripe	mire	quite	pride	click	strike
snipe	smite	squire	vice	lick	ride
stripe	spite	spike	trice	stick	wide

Lesson VII.

Examples of the formation of the plural from the singular, and of other derivatives.

name,	names	camp,	camps	slave,	slaves
dame,	dames	clamp,	clamps	brave,	braves
gale,	gales	lamp,	lamps	stave,	staves

An Easy Standard of Pronunciation.

scale,	scales	scalp,	scalps	mate,	mates
cape,	capes	map,	maps	state,	states
grape,	grapes	plant,	plants	mind,	minds
crane,	cranes	plank,	planks	bind,	binds
shade,	shades	flag,	flags	snare,	snares
grade,	grades	bank,	banks	snake,	snakes

LESSON VIII.

cake,	cakes	chap,	chaps	shake,	shakes
flake,	flakes	flank,	flanks	spade,	spades
hope,	hopes	shine,	shines	pipe,	pipes
note,	notes	slope,	slopes	wire,	wires
blot,	blots	fold,	folds	hive,	hives
cube,	cubes	club,	clubs	pine,	pines
grave,	graves	vote,	votes	fade,	fades
street,	streets	cone,	cones	mill,	mills
sheet,	sheets	bone,	bones	hill,	hills

LESSON IX.

side,	sides	blank,	blanks	mare,	mares
vale,	vales	choke,	chokes	tare,	tares
wife,	wives	cloke,	clokes	grate,	grates
life,	lives	smoke,	smokes	smite,	smites
hive,	hives	flame,	flames	brick,	bricks
drive,	drives	frame,	frames	kick,	kicks
go,	goes	stand,	stands	stick,	sticks
wo,	woes	drove,	droves	bride,	brides
do,	does	robe,	robes	fire,	fires
add,	adds	spot,	spots	smell,	smells
lad,	lads	flag,	flags	swim,	swims

TABLE IV.

Easy words of two syllables, accented on the first.

When the stress of voice falls on a vowel, it is necessarily long,
and is marked by the figure 1. When the stress of voice falls
on a consonant, the preceding vowel is necessarily short, and
is marked by figure 2.

An Easy Standard of Pronunciation.

No figures are placed over the vowels in unaccented syllables,
because they are short. It must be observed, however, that in
unaccented terminating syllables, almost all vowels are pronounced like *i* and *u* short. Thus,

al *is pronounced* ul, *rural*, *rur*ul,
et   it, *fillet*, *fill*it.

This is the general rule in the language; originating doubtless
from this cause, that short *i* and *u* are pronounced with a less
aperture or opening of the mouth, with less exertions of the organs, and consequently with more ease, than the other vowels in
these terminating syllables: for in order to pronounce them right,
nothing more is requisite than to lay a proper stress of the voice
on the accented syllable, and pronounce the unaccented syllables
with more ease and rapidity. When any of these terminations
are accented, as some of them are, the vowel retains its own
sound; as, *compel*, *lament*, *depress*, &c.

The figures are placed over the vowels of the accented syllables; and 'one figure marks all the words that follow till it is
contradicted by another figure.

Bá ker	glo ry	ne gro	sa cred
bri er	gi ant	o ver	se cret
ci der	gra vy	pa gan	sha dy
cra zy	gru el	pa per	si lent
cri er	ho ly	pa pist	so ber
cru el	hu man	pi lot	spi der
di al	i cy	pli ant	sto ry
di et	i dol	po et	stu dent
du ty	i vy	pre cept	stu pid
dy er	ju ry	pru dent	ta per
dra per	ju lep	qui et	tra der
fa tal	la dy	ra ker	ti dings
fe ver	la zy	re al	to ry
fi nal	le gal	ri der	to tal
fla grant	li ar	ri ot	tri al
flu ent	li on	ru by	tru ant
fo cus	ma ker	ru in	tu mult
fru gal	mo dish	ru ler	tu tor
fu el	mo ment	ru ral	va cant

An Easy Standard of Pronunciation.

va grant	cut ler	ham let	mut ter
va ry	dan ger	han sel	num ber
vi per	dif fer	hap py	nut meg
vi tal	din ner	hin der	nurs ling
vo cal	drum mer	hun dred	pam per
wa fer	el der	hunt er	pan nel
wa ges	em bers	in sect	pan try
wa ger	em blem	in step	pat tern
wo ful	en ter	in to	pat ron
åb bot	fac tor	jest er	pen cil
act or	fag got	ken nel	pen ny
ad der	fan cy	kind red	pep per
ad vent	fan tom	king dom	pil lar
al um	fat ling	kins man	pil fer
am ber	fer ret	lad der	pil grim
an gel	fil let	lan tern	plum met
bal lad	flan nel	lap pet	pup py
bank er	flat ter	lat ter	ram mer
ban ter	flut ter	let ter	ran som
bap tist	fran tic	lim ber	rec tor
bat ter	fun nel	lim ner	rem nant
bet ter	gal lop	lit ter	ren der
bit ter	gam mon	luck y	ren net
blun der	gan der	mam mon	rub bish
buf fet	gar ret	man na	sad ler
bur gess	gen try	man ner	sal lad
car rot	gib bet	mat ron	sand y
chan nel	gip sy	mem ber	sat in
chap man	glim mer	mer ry	scan dal
chap ter	glit ter	mill er	scat ter
chat ter	gul let	mit ten	sel dom
chil dren	gun ner	mur der	self ish
chil ly	gus set	mud dy	sen tence
cin der	gut ter	mur mur	shat ter

An Easy Standard of Pronunciation.

shep herd	tan ner	wed ding	hor rid
shil ling	tat ler	wil ful	joc ky
sig nal	tem per	will ing	jol ly
sil ver	ten der	wis dom	mot to
sin ner	ten dril	årt less	on set
slat tern	ten ter	art ist	of fer
slen der	tim ber	af ter	of fice
slum ber	trench er	chŏp per	pot ter
smug gler	trump et	com ment	rob ber
spin net	tum bler	com mon	sot tish
spir it	tur ky	con duct	clĕr gy
splen did	vel lum	con cord	er rand
splen dor	vel vet	con gress	her mit
splin ter	ves sel	con quest	ker nel
stam mer	vic tim	con sul	mer cy
sub ject	vul gar	con vert	per fect
sud den	ug ly	doc tor	per son
suf fer	ul cer	dross y	ser mon
sul len	un der	dol lar	ser pent
sul try	up per	fod der	serv ant
sum mon	ut most	fol ly	ver min
tal ly	ut ter	fop pish	ven om

TABLE V.

Easy words of two syllables, accented on the second.

N. B. In general, when a vowel in an unaccented syllable, stands alone or ends a syllable,* it has its first sound, as in *protect*; yet as we do not dwell upon the vowel, it is short and weak. When the vowel, in such syllables, is joined to a consonant, it has its second sound; as in *address*.

* But if a vowel unaccented ends the word, it has its second sound, as in *city*.

A båse	a like	a maze	at tire
a bide	al lude	as pire	be fore
a dore	a lone	a tone	be have

An Easy Standard of Pronunciation.

be hold	fore seen	trans late	di rect
com ply	im brue	**un** bind	dis band
com pute	im pale	un told	dis miss
com plete	in cite	un fold	dis sent
con fine	in flame	un glue	dis tinct
con jure	in trude	un kind	dis trust
con sume	in sure	un lace	dis tract
con trol	in vite	un ripe	dis turb
cre ate	mis name	un safe	ef fect
de cide	mis place	ab rupt	e mit
de clare	mis rule	ab surd	en camp
de duce	mis take	ac cept	en rich
de fy	mo rose	ad dict	e vent
de fine	par take	ad dress	e vince
de grade	per spire	ad mit	ful fil
de note	po lite	a mend	fi nance
de pute	pre pare	a midst	gal lant
de rive	pro mote	ar range	him self
dis like	re bate	as cend	im pend
dis place	re buke	be set	im plant
dis robe	re cite	ca nal	im press
dis taste	re cline	col lect	im print
di vine	re duce	com pel	in cur
e lope	re late	con duct	in dent
en dure	re ly	con tend	in fect
en force	re mind	con tent	in fest
en gage	re plete	cor rect	in flict
en rage	re vere	cor rupt	in stil
en rol	se duce	de duct	in struct
en sue	sub lime	de fect	in vest
en tice	su pine	de fend	mis give
en tire	su preme	de press	mis print
e vade	sur vive	de range	mis trust
for sworn	tra duce	de tect	mo lest

An Easy Standard of Pronunciation.

neg lect	re press	un bend	re volve
ob struct	re tract	un fit	re volt
oc cur	re trench	un hinge	de spond
of fence	ro bust	un hurt	un lock
o mit	ro mance	un man	con cert
op press	se dan	de bar	de fer
per mit	se lect	de part	di vert
por tend	sub ject	dis arm	in verse
pre tend	sub mit	dis card	in vert
pre dict	sub tract	em balm	per vert
pro ject	sus pense	em bark	per verse
pro tect	trans act	en chant	re fer
pro test	trans cend	en large	con fer
re cant	trans gress	huz za	de ter
re fit	trans plant	un arm	in fer
re lax	tre pan	un bar	in ter
re mit	un apt	ab hor	in tend

TABLE VI.

Easy words of three syllables; the full accent on the first, and a weak accent on the third.

Cru ci fix	lu na cy	si mo ny	ad a mant
cru el ty	no ta ry	stu pi fy	am i ty
de cen cy	nu mer al	tu te lar	am nes ty
di a dem	nu tri ment	va can cy	ar ro gant
di a lect	o ver plus	va gran cy	bar ris ter
dra pe ry	po et ry	ab do men	but ter y
droll e ry	pri ma cy	al le gro	ben e fit
du ti ful	pri ma ry	ad mi ral	big a my
flu en cy	pu ri ty	al co ran	big ot ry
i ro ny	re gen cy	an i mal	but ter fly
i vo ry	ru di ment	an nu al	cal i co
la zi ness	se cre cy	ac ci dent	cal en dar
li bra ry	scru ti ny	al i ment	cab in et

An Easy Standard of Pronunciation.

can is ter	en ti ty	len i ty	ped i gree
can ni bal	ep i gram	lep ro sy	pen al ty
can o py	es cu lent	lev i ty	pen u ry
cap i tal	ev e ry	lib er al	pes ti lent
chast i ty	fac ul ty	lib er ty	pil lo ry
cin na mon	fac to ry	lig a ment	prac tic al
cit i zen	fam i ly	lin e al	prin cip al
clar i fy	fel o ny	lit a ny	pub lic an
clas sic al	fes tiv al	lit er al	punc tu al
clem en cy	fin ic al	lit ur gy	pun gen cy
cler ic al	fish er y	lux u ry	pyr a mid
cur ren cy	gal lant ry	man i fest	rad i cal
cyl in der	gal le ry	man i fold	rar i ty
den i zen	gar ri son	man ner ly	reg u lar
det ri ment	gen er al	mar in er	rem e dy
dif fid ent	gun ner y	med ic al	rib ald ry
dif fer ent	hap pi ness	mel o dy	rev er end
dif fi cult	her ald ry	mem o ry	rit u al
dig ni ty	im ple ment	mes sen ger	riv u let
dil i gent	im pu dent	mil lin er	sac ra ment
div id end	in cre ment	min er al	sal a ry
dul cim er	in di go	min is ter	sat is fy
ec sta cy	in dus try	mus cu lar	sec u lar
ed it or	in fan cy	mys te ry	sed i ment
ef fi gy	in fant ry	nat u ral	sen a tor
el e ment	in fi del	pan o ply	sen ti ment
el e gy	in stru ment	par a dox	sen tin el
em bas sy	in te ger	par a gon	sev er al
eb o ny	in tel lect	par al lax	sil la bub
em bry o	in ter est	par al lel	sim il ar
em e rald	in ter val	par a pet	sin gu lar
em pe ror	in va lid	par i ty	sin is ter
en e my	jus ti fy	pat ri ot	slip pe ry
en mi ty	leg a cy	ped ant ry	sub si dy

An Easy Standard of Pronunciation.

sum ma ry	ur gen cy	hos pi tál	prod i gal
sup ple ment	wag gon er	lot te ry	prod i gy
sym me try	wil der ness	mon u ment	prom in ent
tam a rind	hår bin ger	nom in al	prop er ty
tap es try	har mo ny	oc u lar	pros o dy
tem po ral	harp si chord	oc cu py	prot est ant
ten den cy	côd i cil	of fi cer	quad ru ped
ten e ment	col o ny	or a tor	qual i ty
ter ri fy	com e dy	or i gin	quan ti ty
tes ta ment	com ic al	or na ment	quan da ry
tit u lar	con ju gal	or re ry	cër ti fy
typ ic al	con tin ent	ot to man	mer cu ry
tyr an ny	con tra band	pol i cy	per fi dy
vag a bond	con tra ry	pol i tic	per ju ry
van i ty	doc u ment	pop u lar	per ma nent
vic tór y	drop sic al	pov er ty	per tin ent
vil la ny	glob u lar	pon der ous	reg u late
vin e gar	gloss a ry	prob i ty	ter ma gant

TABLE VII.

*Easy words of three syllables, accented on the
second.*

A båse ment	de co rum	im pru dent
a gree ment	de ni al	oc ta vo
al li ance	de cri al	op po nent
al lure ment	de port ment	po ma tum
ap pa rent	de po nent	pri me val
ar ri val	dic ta tor	re ci tal
a maze ment	di plo ma	re li ance
a tone ment	en rol ment	re qui tal
co e qual	en tice ment	re vi val
con fine ment	e qua tor	spec ta tor
con trol ler	he ro ic	sub scri ber
de ci pher	il le gal	sur vi vor

An Easy Standard of Pronunciation.

tes ta tor	di min ish	pro tect or
tes tă trix	dis sent er	pu is sant
trans la tor	dis tem per	re dund ant
trans pa rent	dis tin guish	re fresh ment
tri bu nal	di ur nal	re lin quish
ver ba tim	dog mat ic	re luct ant
vol ca no	do mes tic	re mem ber
un e qual	dra mat ic	re plen ish
un mind ful	e ject ment	re plev in
a băn don	em bar rass	re pug nant
ac cus tom	em bel lish	re pub lish
af fect ed	em pan nel	ro man tic
ag gress or	en camp ment	se ques ter
a mend ment	e quip ment	spe cif ic
ap par el	er rat ic	sur ren der
ap pend ix	es tab lish	to bac co
as cend ant	hys ter ic	trans cend ent
as sas sin	in ces sant	trans gress or
as sem bly	in clem ent	tri umph ant
at tach ment	in cum bent	um brel la
at tend ant	in hab it	a bŏl ish
be gin ning	in sip id	ăc com plish
be wil der	in trin sic	ad mon ish
co hab it	in val id	as ton ish
col lect or	ma lig nant	de mol ish
con sid er	mo nas tic	dis solv ent
con tin gent	noc tur nal	im mod est
con tract or	pa cif ic	im mor tal
de cant er	pe dant ic	im pos tor
de lin quent	po lem ic	im prop er
de liv er	pre cept or	in con stant
de mer it	pre tend er	in sol vent
de tach ment	pro hib it	im mor al
di lem ma	pro lif ic	un god ly

An Easy Standard of Pronunciation.

TABLE VIII,

Easy words of three syllables, accented on the first and third.

Al a mode	o ver take	in cor rect
dev o tee	rec on cile	in ter mix
dis a gree	ref u gee	o ver run
dis es teem	su per sede	o ver turn
dom i neer	su per scribe	rec ol lect
im ma ture	vol un teer	rec om mend
im por tune	un der mine	rep re hend
in com mode	ap pre hend	su per add
in ter cede	con de scend	un der stand
in tro duce	con tra dict	un der sell
mis ap ply	dis pos sess	un con cern
mis be have	in di rect	dis con nect

TABLE IX.

Easy words of four syllables, the full accent on the first, and the half accent on the third.

Lu mi na ry	dil a to ry	preb end a ry
mo ment a ry	ep i lep sy	pref a to ry
nu ga to ry	em is sa ry	pur ga to ry
bre vi a ry	ig no min y	sal u ta ry
ac cu ra cy	in ti ma cy	sanc tu a ry
ac ri mo ny	in tri ca cy	sec re ta ry
ad mi ral ty	in vent o ry	sed en ta ry
ad ver sa ry	man da to ry	stat u a ry
al i mo ny	mat ri mo ny	sump tu a ry
al le go ry	mer ce na ry	ter ri to ry
cer e mo ny	mis cel la ny	tes ti mo ny
cus tom a ry	mil i ta ry	trib u ta ry
del i ca cy	pat ri mo ny	per emp to ry
dif fi cul ty	plan et a ry	sub lu na ry

An Easy Standard of Pronunciation.

con tro ver sy	prom on to ry	con tu ma cy
mon as te ry	vol un ta ry	con tu me ly
ob sti na cy	ob du rà cy	drom e da ry
prom is so ry	com ment a ry	com mis sa ry

The words het-e-ro-dox, lin-e-a-ment, pat-ri-ot-ism, sep-tu-a-gint, have the full accent on the first syllable, and the half accent on the last.

TABLE X

Easy words of four syllables, accented on the second.

A è ri al	ob scu ri ty	cap tiv i ty
an nu i ty	ob tain a ble	ce lib a cy
ar mo ri al	pro pri e ty	ci vil i ty
cen tu ri on	se cu ri ty	cli mac ter ic
col le gi al	so bri e ty	co in ci dent
com mu ni cant	va cu i ty	col lat e ral
com mu ni ty	va ri e ty	com par is on
con gru i ty	ab surd i ty	com pet it or
con nu bi al	ac tiv i ty	com pul so ry
cor po re al	ac cess a ry	con jec tur al
cre du li ty	ac cess o ry	con spir a cy
cri te ri on	ad min is ter	con stit u ent
e le gi ac	ad vers i ty	de cliv i ty
fu tu ri ty	a dul te ry	de lin quen cy
gram ma ri an	af fin i ty	de prav i ty
gra tu i ty	a nal o gy	di am e ter
his to ri an	a nat o my	dis par i ty
li bra ri an	an tag o nist	di vin i ty
ma te ri al	ar til le ry	ef fect u al
ma tu ri ty	a vid i ty	e lec tric al
me mo ri al	bar bar i ty	em pyr e al
mer cu ri al	bru tal i ty	e pis co pal
out rage ous ly	ca lam i ty	e pit o me

An Easy Standard of Pronunciation.

e quiv a lent	no bil i ty	ve nal i ty
e quiv o cal	nu mer ic al	vi cin i ty
e van gel ist	om nip o tent	a pol o gy
e vent u al	par tic u lar	a pos ta cy
fa tal i ty	per pet u al	as trol o gy
fer til i ty	po lit ic al	as tron o my
fes tiv i ty	po lyg a my	bi og ra phy
fi del i ty	pos ter i ty	com mod i ty
for mal i ty	pre cip it ant	con com it ant
fru gal i ty	pre dic a ment	de moc ra cy
gram mat ic al	pro fund i ty	de spond en cy
ha bit u al	pros per i ty	e con o my
hos til i ty	ra pid i ty	ge om e try
hu man i ty	re cip ro cal	hy poc ri sy
hu mil i ty	re pub lic an	ma jor i ty
i den ti ty	sab bat ic al	me trop o lis
im mens i ty	sa tan ic al	mi nor i ty
im ped i ment	scur ril i ty	mo nop o ly
ju rid ic al	se ver i ty	pre dom in ate
le vit ic al	sig nif ic ant	pri or i ty
lon gev i ty	se ren i ty	tau tol o gy
ma lev o lent	sin cer i ty	ver bos i ty
ma lig ni ty	so lem ni ty	ad ver si ty
mil len ni um	su prem a cy	di ver si ty
mo ral i ty	ter res tri al	e ter ni ty
mu nif i cent	tran quil li ty	hy per bo le
na tiv i ty	ty ran nic al	pro verb i al
ne ces si ty	va lid i ty	sub serv i ent

TABLE XI.

Easy words of four syllables: the full accent on the third, and the half accent on the first.

An te ce dent	com ment a tor
ap par ra tus	me di a tor

An Easy Standard of Pronunciation.

sa cer do tal	mem o ran dum
su per vi sor	o ri ent al
ac ci dĕnt al	or na ment al
ar o mat ic	pan e gyr ic
cal i man co	pred e ces sor
det ri ment al	sci en tif ic
en er get ic	sys tem at ic
fun da ment al	cor res pŏnd ent
in nu en do	hor i zon tal
mal e fac tor	ŭ ni vĕr sal
man i fest o	un der stand ing
at mos pher ic	o ver whelm ing

☞ Having proceeded through tables composed of easy words, from one to four syllables, let the learner begin the following tables, which consist of more difficult words. In these the child will be much assisted by a knowledge of the figures, and the use of the Italics.

If the Instructor should think it useful to let his pupils read some of the easy lessons before they have finished spelling, he may divide their studies—let them spell one part of the day, and read the other

- - -

TABLE XII.

Difficult and irregular Monosyllables.

I would recommend this table to be read sometimes across the page.

Bày	clay	rail	flail	brain
day	way	frail	snail	chain
hay	ray	wail	laird	grain
lay	pray	mail	aid	slain
say	stray	mail	maid	train
may	slay	trail	stair	rain
pay	spay	bail	swear	main
pray	jail	ail	wear	plain
sway	pail	hail	bear	sprain
fray	sail	tail	tear	stain

An Easy Standard of Pronunciation.

twain	tray	change	squeal	creed
vain	gay	strange	beer	heed
wain	slay	blaze	peer	mead
paint	play	be	deer	knead
quaint	beard	pea	fear	reed
plaint	date	sea	dear	bleed
aim	tale	tea	hear	bread
claim	staid	flea	near	plead
main	laid	yea	rear	deem
waif	paid	key	veer	seem
stage	braid	leap	drear	cream
gauge	air	neap	clear	dream
plague	chair	reap	shear	stream
vague	fair	cheap	steer	beam
bait	hair	heap	bier	steam
great	pair	steel	tier	seam
gait	lain	kneel	year	gleam
wait	pain	teal	cheer	scream
plait	strain	feel	heard	fleam
strait	gain	keel	blear	fream
graze	blain	deal	ear	ream
praise	drain	heal	sear	team
raise	fain	meal	smear	least
baise	faint	peel	spear	feast
raze	taint	reel	tear	yeast
maize	saint	seal	queer	beast
shave	trait .	steal	deed	priest
brave	haste	veal	feed	east
knave	paste	weal	need	reef
break	waste	zeal	weed	grief
steak	baste	peal	bead	brief
spray	chaste	beal	lead	chief
stay	taste	ceil	read	deaf
gray	traipse	cel	seed	leaf

An Easy Standard of Pronunciation.

sheaf	teat	sleeve	league	sleight
fief	beak	grieve	teague	bright
lief	leak	reeve	tweag	fight
beef	weak	leave	leash	blight
plea	bleak	lieve	liege	fright
flee	sneak	reave	siege	flight
bee	speak	beeves	dry	wight
deep	freak	eaves	bye	wright
keep	squeak	greaves	fly	clime
weep	reek	freeze	cry	rhyme
steep	cheek	sneeze	sky	knife
sleep	wreak	breeze	lie	climb
creep	fleak	ease	die	smile
sheep	screak	squeeze	eye	stile
fleece	shriek	cheese	buy	guile
peace	sleek	frieze	try	mild
cease	streak	please	fry	child
lease	seen	seize	pie	wild
geese	bean	tease	wry	bride
niece	clean	speech	high	stride
piece	mien	leach	nigh	guide
grease	queen	beach	sigh	guise
crease	wean	reach	by	fro
meet	keen	teach	fie	doe
bleat	glean	screech	hie	toe
cheat	spleen	breach	vie	foe
treat	dean	bleach	light	bow
meat	green	eacn	might	mow
seat	quean	peach	height	tow
feat	yean	fiend	night	row
beat	lean	yield	right	owe
neat	mean	shield	sight	flow
feet	heave	wield	tight	glow
heat	cleave	field	slight	blow

An Easy Standard of Pronunciatio.

slow	róast	loan	hoarse	me
know	coast	shown	source	shrew
grow	toast	old	coarse	spew
snow	more	told	board	stew
stow	four	cold	hoard	tew
strow	pour	mold	gourd	yew
dough	door	port	sword	chew
hoe	floor	fort	holme	clew
sloe	roar	sport	oaf	ewe
mole	boar	court	loaf	slue
pole	hoar	goad	due	mew
sole	oar	load	true	cure
foal	soar	toad	you	pure
goat	oat	woad	glue	your
roll	boat	soap	sue	rude
poll	doat	froze	dew	prude
boll	goat	close	few	shrewd
toll	moat	prose	pew	crude
soul	bloat	chose	new	feud
scroll	float	coach	lieu	rheum
coal	joke	poach	view	muse
shoal	oak	roach	flew	bruise
bowl	croak	broach	grew	use
knoll	cloke	folks	screw	cruise
stroll	soak	coax	brew	spruce
troll	tone	foam	blew	use
brogue	own	roam	drew	juice
rogue	known	comb	knew	cruse
vogue	groan	loam	crew	sluice
most	blown	shorn	hew	fruit
post	flown	sworn	strew	bruit
host	mówn	mourn	shew	suit
boast	sown	force	slew	mewl
ghost	moan	course	blue	lure

An Easy Standard of Pronunciation.

.10	check	delve	skill	jolt
lamb	speck	valve	spill	boult
plaid	wreck	guess	chill	dolt
limb	meant	breast	ditch	moult
gaunt	sense	guest	pitch	coat
dense	tense	sweat	witch	dost
hence	bench	debt	twitch	curl
pence	clench	stem	niche	hurl
fence	stench	phlegm	hinge	churl
lapse	quench	wink	singe	drum
flat	wench	pink	cringe	dumb
gnat	wrench	cinque	fringe	crumb
cash	drench	prism	twinge	numb
clash	fetch	schism	glimpse	plum
gnash	sketch	chip	since	much
strap	wretch	skip	rinse	such
wrap	spend	ship	wince	touch
shall	friend	strip	teint	crutch
bled	blend	scrip	brick	burst
dead	badge	spin	stick	stuff
stead	fadge	chin	kick	snuff
read	edge	twin	wick	rough
tread	hedge	skin	quick	tough
bread	wedge	guilt	spit	plump
dread	sledge	built	knit	stump
spread	ledge	quilt	twit	trump
shred	sedge	build	live	lurch
head	pledge	drift	sieve	church
cleanse	dredge	shift	ridge	young
realm	fledge	swift	none	gulf
dram	bridge	twist	stone	nymph
deck	bilge	wrist	home	hymn
neck	helve	risk	bolt	judge
peck	twelve	shr !	colt	grudge

An Easy Standard of Pronunciation.

drudge	lost	sawn	squall	cough
trudge	tost	brawn	yawl	trough
shrub	war	spawn	awl	fork
scrub	fort†	yawn	haul	cork
bulge	nort†	laud	stall	hawk
gurge	taught	fraud	small	balk
surge	caught	broad	crawl	walk
purge	brought	cord	brawl	talk
plunge	sought	lord	bawl	chalk
curse	ought	ward	caul	stalk
purse	wrought	gauze	drawl	calk
law	fought	cause	wart	daub
shaw	groat	pause	sort	bawd
taw	fraught	clause	short	warp
maw	naught	torch	quart	wasp
raw	form	scorch	snort	want
paw	storm	gorge	bald	sauce
saw	swarm	all	scald	balm
awe	warm	tall	off	calm
gnaw	born	fall	oft	palm
straw	corn	hall	loft	psalm
flaw	warn	gall	soft	qualm
draw	corse	pall	cross	alms
chaw	horn	ball	dross	bask
claw	morn	call	moss	cask
craw	fawn	wall	loss	ask
haw	lawn	maul	horse	mask
jaw	dawn	scrawl	corpse	task
cost*	pawn	sprawl	dwarf	ark

* Perhaps *o* and *a* in the words *cost, born, warm,* &c. may be considered as coming more properly under the figure 5. But the liquids that follow them, have such an effect in lengthening the syllable, that it appears more natural to place them under figure 3. A similar remark applies to *a* in *bar*.

† These words, when unemphatical, are necessarily sharp.

An Easy Standard of Pronunciation.

bark	starve	daunt	gap	knock
dark	arm	flaunt	carp	drop
hark	harm	haunt	darn	crop
mark	charm	jaunt	barn	shop
lark	farm	taunt	yarn	shock
park	barm	vaunt	bar	wan
spark	art	cast	fär	swan
arc	cart	past	scar	gone
shark	dart	last	spar	wash
stark	hart	vast	star	swash
asp	mart	blast	tar	watch
clasp	part	fast	czar	was
hasp	tart	mast	car	wast
rasp	start	mass	char	knob
gasp	smart	pass	jar	swab
grasp	chart	lass	mar	wad
hard	heart	bass	par	dodge
bard	staff	brass	barb	lodge
card	chaff	class	garb	bodge
lard	half	glass	carle	podge
guard	calf	grass	marl	fosse
pard	laugh	arch	snarl	bond
yard	craft	march	chance	fond
branch	shaft	parch	dance	pond
lanch	waft	starch	prance	wand
staunch	raft	harsh	lance	strong
haunch	draught	charge	glance	wrong
blanch	aft	large	trance	botch
craunch	haft	barge	scarf	scotch
carp	pant	farce	laste	mosque
harp	grant	parse	swåp	blot
sharp	slant	calve.	dock	yacht
scarp	ant	halve	mock	scoat
carve	aunt	salve	clock	halt

An Easy Standard of Pronunciation.

salt	spool	woo	roof	stirp
malt	droop	proof	loof	chirp
fault	scoop	woof	soon	jerk
vault	troop	loose	hoop†	perk
false	loop	goose	coop	smerk
bronze	soup	moose	poop	yerk
doom	group	spoon	full	quirk
room	hoop*	roost	bull	herb
boom	boot	root	pull	verb
loom	coot	foot	wool	fir
bloom	hoot	shoot	bush	myrrh
groom	toot	book	push	fern
womb	moot	cook	puss	earn
tomb	food	hook	earl	yearn
broom	rood	look	pearl	learn
spoon	brood	took	skirt‡	stern
boon	mood	brook	verse	kern
moon	move	crook	fierce	quern
noon	prove	flook	pierce	search
loon	groove	rook	tierce	perch
swoon	noose	shook	herse	swerve
bourn	choose	croup	terse	wert
poor	lose	wood	verge	son
tour	booze	stood	serge	run
moor	ooze	good	dirge	ton
boor	ouse	hood	virge	won
cool	coo	could	vert	done
fool	two	would	term	one§
tool	do	should	firm	come
stool	shoe	wolf	germ	some
pool	loo	hoof	sperm	bomb

* To cry out.   † Of a cask.
‡ Under this figure in the words *skirt*, &c. *i* has the sound of second *e*.
§ Pronounced wun.

An Easy Standard of Pronunciation.

clomb	once*	foil	brow	browse
rhomb	monk	boil	plow	spouse
dirt	tongue	coil	bough	drowse
shirt	birch	join	slough	cloud
flirt	sponge	coin	out	crowd
wort	heir	loin	stout	loud
girt	trey	groin	oust	proud
spirt	sley	boy	trout	shroud
squirt	prey	joy	gout	bound
kirk	grey	toy	pout	hound
work	weigh	coy	clout	,pound
bird	cigh	cloy	rout	round
word	neigh	buoy	shout	sound
first	reign	point	spout	ground
worst	vein	joint	scout	wound
worse	feign	voice	doubt	foul
blood	deign	choice	bout	bowl
flood	skein	moist	drought	fowl
sir	rein	hoist	our	scowl
her	eight	joist	sour	cowl
stir	freight	noise	brown	growl
worm	weight	quoit	crown	howl
world	streight	coif	down	bounce
front	tete	quoif	drown	ounce
ront	feint	*ou* and *ow*	frown	pounce
wont	veil	now	clown	flounce
dove	*oi* and *oy*	cow	gown	couch
love	oil	how	town	vouch
shove	spoil	bow	house	slouch
glove	soil	mow	louse	pouch
twirl	broil	sow	mouse	gouge
dunce	toil	vow	douse	lounge

* Pronounced wunce.

An Easy Standard of Pronunciation.

MONOSYLLABLES IN *TH.*

The following have the first sound of th, *viz. as in* thick, thin.

Thròw	thowl	hath	breadth	bath
truth	threw	rath	filth	lath
youth	thrice	pith	frith	wrath
sheath	thrive	with*	plinth	thròb
heath	throne	theft	spilth	throng
both	throe	thatch	thâw	thong
oath	throve	thill	cloth	tôoth
forth	thing	third	moth	through
fourth	think	thrill	broth	èarth
highth	thin	thrush	sloth	dearth
three	thank	thwak	troth	birth
throat	thick	tilth	north	girth
theme	thrift	withe	loth	mirth
thigh	thumb	doth	thought	third
thief	thump	smith	thorn	thirst
faith	length	thrust	froth	worth
bloweth	strength	thrum	thrall	month
growth	breath	thread	thwart	thirl
quoth	death	stealth	warmth	ou
ruth	health	thrash	swath	south
teeth	wealth	depth	pâth	mouth
thane	threat	width	hearth	drouth

---

* In this word, *th* has its first sound before a consonant, as in *withstand*; and its second sound before a vowel, as in *without*, *with us.* But in other compound words, *th* generally retains the sound of its primitive.

An Easy Standard of Pronunciation.

The following have the second sound of th, *as in* thou.

Thine	teeth*	blithe	then	soothe
thy	those	wreath	thus	they
bathe	tithe	writhe	the	there
lathe	these	sythe	them	their
swathe	though	seethe	thence	*ou*
clothe	thee	breathe	than	thou
loathe	hithe	this	booth	mouth
meethe	lithe	that	smooth	

* The noun *teeth*, has the first sound of *th*, and the verb to *teeth* its second sound. The same is observable of *mouth* and to *mouth*. This is the reason why these words are found under both heads.

The words *mouth, moth, cloth, oath, path, swath, bath, lath*, have the first sound of *th* in the singular number, and the second in the plural.

Examples of the formation of plurals, and other derivatives.

Bay,	bays	stain,	stains	saint,	saints
day,	days	brain,	brains	heap,	heaps
lay,	lays	chain,	chains	tear,	tears
pay,	pays	pain,	pains	hear,	hears
pray,	prays	paint,	paints	spear,	spears
sway,	sways	claim,	claims	creed,	creeds
way,	ways	strait,	straits	trait,	traits
mail,	mails	plague,	plagues	chief,	chiefs
nail,	nails	key,	keys	leak,	leaks
sail,	sails	knave,	knaves	speak,	speaks
weep,	weeps	green,	greens	sheaf,	sheaves
seam,	seams	yield,	yields	leaf,	leaves
fly,	flies	stride,	strides	poll,	polls
cry,	cries	guide,	guides	soul,	souls
dry,	dries	smile,	smiles	coal,	coals

An Easy Standard of Pronunciation.

sky,	skies	toe,	toes	bowl,	bowls
buy,	buys	foe,	foes	rogue,	rogues
sigh,	sighs	bow,	bows	post,	posts
flight,	flights	glow,	glows	host,	hosts
light,	lights	flow,	flows	toast,	toasts
sight,	sights	blow,	blows	coast,	coasts
life,	lives	snow,	snows	door,	doors
wife,	wives	hoe,	hoes	floor,	floors
knife,	knives	foal,	foals	oar,	oars

TABLE XIII.

Lessons of easy words, to teach children to read, and to know their duty.

Lesson I.

No man may put off the law of God :
My joy is in his law all the day.
O may I not go in the way of sin !
Let me not go in the way of ill men.

II.

A bad man is a foe to the law :
It is his joy to do ill.
All men go out of the way.
Who can say he has no sin ?

III.

The way of man is ill.
My son, do as you are bid :
But if you are bid, do no ill.
See not my sin, and let me not go to the pit.

IV.

Rest in the Lord, and mind his word.
My son, hold fast the law that is good.
You must not tell a lie, nor do hurt.
We must let no man hurt us.

V.

Do as well as you can, and do no harm.
Mark the man that doth well, and do so too.
Help such as want help, and be kind.
Let your sins past put you in mind to mend.

VI.

I will not walk with bad men, that I may not
    be cast off with them.
I will love the law and keep it.
I will walk with the just and do good.

VII.

This life is not long; but the life to come has
    no end.
We must pray for them that hate us.
We must love them that love not us.
We must do as we like to be done to.

VIII.

A bad life will make a bad end.
He must live well that will die well.
He doth live ill that doth not mend.
In time to come we must do no ill.

IX.

No man can say that he has done no ill,
For all men have gone out of the way.
There is none that doetn good; no, not one.
If I have done harm, I must do it no more.

X.

Sin will lead us to pain and wo.
Love that which is good, and shun vice.
Hate no man, but love both friends and foes.
A bad man can take no rest, day nor night.

An Easy Standard of Pronunciation.

XI.

He who came to save us, will wash us from all sin; I will be glad in his name.

A good boy will do all that is just: he will flee from vice; he will do good, and walk in the way of life.

Love not the world, nor the things that are in the world; for they are sin.

I will not fear what flesh can do to me; for my trust is in him who made the world.

He is nigh to them that pray to him, and praise his name.

XII.

Be a good child; mind your book; love your school, and strive to learn.

Tell no tales; call no ill names; you must not lie, nor swear, nor cheat, nor steal.

Play not with bad boys; use no ill words at play; spend your time well; live in peace, and shun all strife. This is the way to make good men love you, and save your soul from pain and woe.

XIII.

A good child will not lie, swear, nor steal.--He will be good at home, and ask to read his book; when he gets up he will wash his hands and face clean; he will comb his hair, and make haste to school; he will not play by the way, as bad boys do.

XIV.

When good boys and girls are at school, they will mind their books, and try to learn to spell and read well, and not play in the time of school.

An Easy Standard of Pronunciation.

When they are at church, they will sit, kneel, or stand still; and when they are at home, will read some good book, that God may bless them.

XV.

As for those boys and girls that mind not their books, and love not the church and school, but play with such as tell tales, tell lies, curse, swear and steal, they will come to some bad end, and must be whipt till they mend their ways.

TABLE XIV.

Words of two syllables accented on the first.

1.	fea ture	ni ter	tai lor
A cre	fe male	oat meal	trai tor
a pron	fro ward	past ry	trea ty
bare foot	grate ful	pi ous	wea ry
beast ly	griev ous	peo ple	wo ful
brew er	gno mon	plu mage	wri ter
beau ty	hein ous	pa rent	wain scot
brok en	hind most	pro logue	yeo man
boat swain	hoar y	quo ta	ab sence
bow sprit	hu mor	rhu barb	ab bey
brave ry	jew el	ri fle	am ple
ca ble	jui cy	rogu ish	asth ma
cheap en	knave ry	re gion	an cle
dai ly	knight hood	sea son	bal ance
dai sy	li ver	spright ly	bel fry
dea con	la bor	sti fle	bash ful
dia mond	le gion	stee ple	bish op
do tage	may or	bol ster	blem ish
eve ning	me ter	coul ter	blus ter
fa vor	mi ter	slave ry	brim stone
fla vor	mea sles	shoul der	brick kiln

An Easy Standard of Pronunciation.

blud geon	dam son	grav el	mel on
bel lows	dan gle	grum ble	mer it
bis cuit	dac tyl	guin ea	min gle
brit tle	debt or	gud geon	mis tress
buck ram	dim ple	hand ful	mis chief
bus tle	dis tance	hab it	musk et
cam el	doub le	has soc	mus lin
cap rice	driv en	hav oc	mus ter
cap tain	dud geon	heif er	mar riage
cen sure	dun geon	heav y	nev er
chap el	drunk ard	hin drance	nim ble
chast en	dust y	hus band	pad lock
cher ish	ec logue	hum ble	pamph let
chim ney	en gine	husk y	pen ance
car ry	en sign	im age	pes ter
car riage	en trails	in stance	phren zy
cis tern	er ror	in ward	pis mire
cit y	fash ion	isth mus	plan et
clam or	fam ish	jeal ous	pleas ant
clean ly	fas set	jour nal	peas ant
cred it	fat ten	judge ment	pinch ers
crev ice	fes ter	knuck le	prat tle
crick et	fer riage	knap sack	pun ish
crust y	fid dle	lan guage	puz zle
crys tal	flag on	lan guor	pic ture
cup board	frec kle	land lord	pur chase
cus tom	frus trate	lev el	prac tice
crib bage	fur lough	lim it	phthis ic
cul ture	fran chise	lus ter	punch eon
cous in	ges ture	lunch eon	quick en
cut lass	gant let	mad am	ram ble
dam age	gin gle	mal ice	rap id
dam ask	glis ten	man gle	rat tle
dam sel	grand eur	mas tiff	reb el

An Easy Standard of Pronunciation.

rel ish	tav ern	daugh ter	mar ket
rig or	tempt er	au tumn	mas ter
ris en	ten ant	fault y	mar quis
riv er	till age	for tress	par cel
riv et	tip ple	for tune	par don
ruf fle	tres pass	gau dy	par lor
res in	troub le	geor gic	part ner
sam ple	twink ling	gorge ous	pas ture
salm on	trans port	lau rel	psalm ist
satch el	trun cheon	lord ship	scar let
scab bard	ven om	haugh ty	slan der
scis sors	ven ture	morn ing	al so
seven night	vint age	mor tal	al way
scep ter	vis it	mort gage	bon fire
spec ter	vis age	naugh ty	cob ler
scrib ble	vict uals	saw yer	clos et
scuf fle	venge ance	tor ment	col league
sin ew	veni son	wa ter	com et
sim ple	vine yard	sau cy	com rade
sin gle	wel come	sau cer	con quer
scep tic	wed lock	an swer	cock swain
smug gle	wick ed	bar ber	con duit
span gle	wran gle	brace let	cop y
spig ot	wrap per	cart er	con trite
spit tle	wres tle	cham ber	cof fin
spin dle	wrist band	craft y	doc trine
sup ple	weap on	char coal	flor id
subt le	wid geon	flask et	fon dle
stur geon	zeal ot	gar land	fore head
sur geon	zeal ous	ghast ly	frol ic
tal ent	zeph yr	gar ment	fal chion
tal on	slaugh ter	har lot	grog ram
tan gle	bor der	har vest	gos lin
tat tle	cor ner	jaun dice	hogs head

An Easy Standard of Pronunciation.

hom·age	spon dee	coop er	shov el
hon est	wan der	cuck oo	squir rel
hon or	wan ton	ver min	ver gin
knowl edge	war rant	ver dict	wor ship
hal loe	squan der	ver juce	won der
lodg er	yon der	vir tue	neigh bor
mod est	gloom y	kern el	ou
mod ern	wo man	con jure	coun cil
mon strous	boo by	hov er	coun ter
nov el	wool len	cir cuit	coun ty
nov ice	bush el	fir kin	dough ty
prof fer	bo som	com pass	drow sy
prog ress	bush y	com fort	mount ain
prom ise	worst ed	bor ough	show er
pros pect	cush ion	dirt y	flow er
pros per	bul let	gov ern	bow er
quad rant	bul lock	hon ey	pow er
quad rate	bul iy	sove reign	oy
squad ron	bul wark	stir rup	voy age
stop page	butch er	skir mism	

TABLE XV.

Lesson I.

THE time will come when we must all be laid in the dust.

Keep thy tongue from ill, and thy lips from guile. Let thy words be plain and true to the thoughts of the heart.

He that strives to vex or hurt those that sit next him, is a bad boy, and will meet with foes let him go where he will; but he that is kind, and loves to live in peace, will make friends of all that know him.

An Easy Standard of Pronunciation.

A clown will not make a bow, nor thank you
when you give him what he wants; but he that is
well bred, will do both.

He that speaks loud in school will not learn his
own book well, nor let the rest learn theirs; but
those that make no noise will soon be wise, and
gain much love and good will.

II.

Shun the boy that tells lies, or speaks bád words;
for he would soon bring thee to shame.

He that does no harm shall gain the love of the
whole school; but he that strives to hurt the rest,
shall gain their ill will.

He that lies in bed when he should go to school,
is not wise: but he that shakes off sleep shall have
praise.

He is a fool that does not choose the best boys
when he goes to play; for bad boys will cheat, and
lie, and swear, and strive to make him as bad as
themselves.

Slight no man, for you know not how soon you
may stand in need of his help.

III.

If you have done wrong, own your fault; for he
that tells a lie to hide it, makes it worse.

He that tells the truth is a wise child; but he
that tells lies, will not be heard when he speaks the
truth.

When you are at school, make no noise, but keep
your seat, and mind your book; for what you learn
will do you good, when you grow to be a man.

Play no tricks on them that sit next you; for if

An Easy Standárd of Pronunciation.

you do, good boys will shun you as they would a dog that they knew would bite them.

He that hurts you at the same time that he calls you his friend, is worse than a snake in the grass.

Be kind to all men, and hurt not thyself.

A wise child loves to learn his book, but the fool would choose to play with toys.

IV.

Sloth keeps such a hold of some boys, that they lie in bed when they should go to school ; but a boy that wants to be wise will drive sleep far from him.

Love him that loves his book, and speaks good words, and does no harm : for such a friend may do thee good all the days of thy life.

Be kind to all as far as you can ; you know not how soon you may want their help ; and he that has the good will of all that know him, shall not want a friend in time of need.

If you want to be good, wise and strong, read with care such books as have been made by wise and good men ; think of what you read in your spare hours; be brisk at play, but do not swear ; and waste not too much of your time in bed.

TABLE XVI.

Words of two syllables accented on the second.

Ac quire	af fair	ap proach	a stray
a base	af fright	ar raign	a vail
a buse	a gainst	a rise	a wake
a dieu	a muse	as sign	a way

An Easy Standard of Pronunciation.

al ly	en croach	un tie	a far
aw ry	en dear	un true	a larm
be lieve	en treat	up right	guit ar
be lief	ex cise	ad journ	in graft
be nign	ex pose	a byss	re mark
be siege	in crease	at tack	sur pass
be low	in dict	at tempt	ca tarrh
be stow	im pair	a venge	re gard
bo hea	in fuse	ad ept	ap prove
con sign	in scribe	be head	a mour
com plain	ma lign	be twixt	bab oon
cam paign	ob tain	bur lesque	bas soon
com pose	o pake	con temn	be hoove
con dign	ob lige	con tempt	buf foon
con cise	per tain	co quet	ca noe
con ceit	pre vail	e nough	car touch
con fuse	pre scribe	fi nesse	dis prove
con strain	pro pose	ga zette	a do
de ceive	pur suit	gro tesque	a loof
de ceit	pro rogue	har angue	e merge
de crease	re ceive	im mense	im merse
de light	re ceipt	qua drille	af firm
de pose	re course	so journ	de sert
de scribe	re pair	be cause	de serve
de sign	re pose	a dorn	a bove
de sire	re prieve	a broad	a mong
de vise	re straint	de fraud	be come
dis claim	re sume	de bauch	be love
dis course	re tain	per form	con vey
dis may	re sign	re ward	sur vey
dis own	sup pose	sub orn	in veigh
dis play	tran scribe	trans form	oi
dis pose	trans pose	e clat	ap point
in close	un close	ad vance	a noint

An Easy Standard of Pronunciation.

a void	re joice	com pound	pro pound
em broil	sub join	con found	sur mount
en joy	dis joint	de vour	al low
de stroy	*ou*	ac count	a bound
de coy	a mount	pro nounce	an nounce
pur loin	a bout	re nounce	ca rouse

TABLE XVII.

Examples of words derived from their roots or primitives.

EXAMPLE I.

Prim.	Deriv.	Prim.	Deriv.	Prim.	Deriv.
Rain,	rain-y	grass,	grass-y	froth,	froth-y
rust,	rust-y	glass,	glass-y	drouth,	drouth-y
leaf,	leaf-y	ice,	i-cy	size,	si-zy
stick,	stick-y	frost,	frost-y	chill,	chill-y
pith,	pith-y	snow,	snow-y	chalk,	chalk-y
length,	length-y	fog,	fog-gy	down,	down-y
slight,	slight-y	wood,	wood-y	gloss,	gloss-y
storm,	storm-y	room,	room-y	worth,	wor-thy

EXAMPLE II.

Plural nouns of two syllables, formed from the singular of one syllable.

lace,	la-ces	brush,	brush-es	house,	hous-es
face,	fa-ces	price,	pri-ces	church,	church-es
pace,	pa-ces	slice,	sli-ces	box,	box-es
trace,	tra-ces	spice,	spi-ces	tierce,	tier-ces
cage,	ca-ges	grace,	gra-ces	verse,	vers-es
page,	pa-ges	press,	press-es	lodge,	lodg-es
nose,	no-ses	dress,	dress-es	watch,	watch-es
rose,	ro-ses	maze,	ma-zes	noise,	nois-es
curse,	curs-es	fish,	fish-es	voice,	voic-es
purse,	purs-es	horse,	hors-es	charge,	charg-es
surge,	surg-es	corpse,	corps-es	sense,	sens-es

An Easy Standard of Pronunciation.

loss,	loss-es	cause,	caus-es	fringe,	frin-ges
arch,	arch-es	farce,	far-ces	ridge,	ridg-es
cheese,	chees-es	course,	cours-es	dance,	dan-ces

EXAMPLE III.

Words formed by adding *ing* to verbs, and called *Participles.*

call,	call-ing	al-lay,	al-lay-ing
air,	air-ing	com-plain,	com-plain-ing
faint,	faint-ing	al-low,	al-low-ing
feel,	feel-ing	fin-ish,	fin-ish-ing
see,	see-ing	lav-ish,	lav-ish-ing
beat,	beat-ing	glim-mer,	glim-mer-ing

Words in which *e* final is omitted in the derivative.

change,	chang-ing	ex-change,	ex-chang-ing
glance,	glanc-ing	dis-pose,	dis-pos-ing
prance,	pranc-ing	gen-er-ate,	gen-e-rat-ing
grace,	grac-ing	con-verse,	con-vers-ing
give,	giv-ing	con-vince,	con-vinc-ing
hedge,	hedg-ing	op-e-rate,	op-e-rat-ing
style,	styl-ing	dis-solve,	dis-solv-ing
solve,	solv-ing	im-i-tate,	im-i-tat-ing
tri-fle,	tri-fling	re-ceive,	re-ceiv-ing
ri-fle,	ri-fling	per-ceive,	per-ceiv-ing
shuf-fle,	shuf-fling	prac-tice,	prac-tic-ing

EXAMPLE IV.

The manner of expressing degrees of comparison in qualities, by adding *er* and *est*, or *r* and *st*; called Positive, Comparative, and Superlative.

Pos.	Comp.	Superl.	Pos.	Comp.	Superl.
great,	great-er,	great-est	wise	wis-er,	wis-est
kind,	kind-er,	kind-est	ripe,	rip-er,	rip-est
bold,	bold-er,	bold-est	rare,	rar-er,	rar-est
rich,	rich-er,	rich-est	grave,	grav-er,	grav-est
near,	near-er,	near-est	chaste,	chast-er,	chast-est
cold,	cold-er,	cold-est	brave,	brav-er,	brav-est
warm,	warm-er,	warm-est	vile,	vil-er,	vil-est

An Easy Standard of Pronunciation.

EXAMPLE V.

Words ending in *ish*, expressing a degree of quality less than the positive

red-dish,	red,	red-der,	red-dest
brown-ish,	brown,	brown-er,	brown-est
whi-tish,	white,	whi-ter,	whi-test
green-ish,	green,	green-er,	green-est
black-ish,	black,	black-er,	black-est
blu-ish,	blue,	blu-er,	blu-est
yel-low-ish,	yel-low,	yel-low-er,	yel-low-est

EXAMPLE VI.

Formation of verbs in the three persons.

Present Time.

Singular number.   *Plural.*

1   2   3

I love, thou lovest, ⎰ he loveth, ⎱ 1 We love
    you love,   ⎱ he loves, ⎰ 2 ye or you love
       she loves, 3 they love
       it loves,

I grant, thou grantest, ⎰ he granteth, ⎱ We grant
    you grant,   ⎱ he grants, ⎰ ye or you grant
       she grants, they grant
       it grants,

Past Time.

I loved, thou lovedst, ⎰ he loved, ⎱ We loved
    you loved,   ⎱ she loved, ⎰ ye or you loved
       it loved, they loved

TABLE XVIII.

Familiar Lessons.

A Dog growls and barks; a cat mews and purrs; a cock crows; a hen clucks and cackles; a bird

An Easy Standard of Pronunciation.

TABLE XVIII.
Familiar Lessons.

A DOG growls and barks; a cat mews and purrs; a cock crows; a hen clucks and cackles; a bird chirps and sings; an ox lows; a bull bellows; a lion roars; a horse neighs; an ass brays; a whale spouts. Birds fly in the air by the help of wings; snakes crawl on the earth without feet; fishes swim in water, by means of fins; beasts have feet, with hoofs or claws, to walk or run on land.

All animals are fitted for certain modes of living. The birds which feed on flesh, have strong claws, to catch and hold small animals, and a hooked bill to tear the flesh in pieces; such is the vulture and the hawk. Fowls which feed on insects and grain, have mostly a short strait bill, like the robin. Those which live on fish, have long legs for wading, or long bills for seizing and holding their prey, like the heron and fish hawk. Fowls which delight chiefly to fly in the air, and light and build nests on the trees, have their toes divided, by which they cling to the branches and twigs; those which live in and about water have webbed feet, that is, their toes united by a film or skin, so that their feet serve as oars or paddles for swimming.

See the dog, the cat, the wolf, the lion, the panther and catamount; what sharp claws and pointed teeth they have, to seize little animals, and tear them in pieces! But see the gentle cow and ox, and timid sheep—these useful animals are made for man,—they have no claws, nor sharp teeth,—they have only blunt teeth in the under jaw, fitted to crop the grass of the field :—they feed in quiet, and come at the call of man. Oxen submit to the yoke, and plow the field, or draw the cart ;—the cow

An Easy Standard of Pronunciation.

returns home at evening, to fill the farmer's pails with milk, the wholesome food of men; and the sheep yields her yearly fleece to furnish us with warm garments.

Henry, tell me the number of days in a year. Three hundred and sixty-five.—How many weeks in a year? Fifty-two.—How many days in a week? Seven.—What are they called? Sunday, Monday, Tuesday, Wednesday, Thursday, Friday, Saturday; Sunday is the Sabbath, or day of rest, and called the Lord's day, being devoted to religious duties.—How many hours are there in a day? Twenty-four.—How many minutes in an hour? Sixty, and sixty seconds in a minute. Time is measured by clocks and watches, dials and glasses. The light of the sun makes the day, and the shade of the earth makes the night. The earth is round, and rolls round from west to east once in twenty-four hours. The day time is for labor, and the night for sleep and repose. Children should go to bed early.

Charles, how is the year divided? Into months and seasons.—How many are the months? Twelve calendar months, and nearly thirteen lunar months. What are the names of the calendar months? January, February, March, April, May, June, July, August, September, October, November, December. January begins the year, and the first day of that month is called New Year's day. Then people express to each other their good wishes, and little boys and girls expect gifts of little books, toys and plums.—What is the lunar month? It is the time from one change of the moon to another, which is about twenty-nine days and a half.

John, what are the seasons? Spring, summer,

An Easy Standard of Pronunciation.

autumn or fall, and winter. · The spring is so called from the springing or first shooting of the plants : when they put forth leaves and blossoms, all nature is decked with bloom, and perfumed with fragrant odors. The spring months are March, April and May. The summer months are June, July and August, when the sun pours his heating rays on the earth, the trees are clothed with leaves and fruit, and the ground is covered with herbage. The autumnal months are September, October and November; which are also called *fall*, from the *fall* of the leaves. Now the fruits are gathered, the verdure of the plants decays; the leaves of the forest turn red or yellow, and fall from the trees, and nature is stripped of her verdant robes. Then comes dreary winter. In December, January and February, frost binds the earth in chains, and spreads an icy bridge over rivers and lakes : the snow with her white mantle enwraps the earth; no birds fill the air with the music of their notes; the beasts stand shivering in the stall ; and men crowd around the fire-side, or wrapped in wool and fur, prepare to meet the chilling blast.

ADVICE.

Prefer solid sense to vain wit ; study to be useful rather than diverting ; commend and respect nothing so much as true piety and virtue—Let no jest intrude to violate good manners ; never utter what may offend the chastest ear.

An Easy Standard of Pronunciation.

TABLE XIX.

Words of three syllables, the full accent on the first, and the half accent on the third.

Note. In half accented terminations, *ate, ude, ure, ize, ute, ise, ule, uge, ide,* the vowel has its first sound generally, though not dwelt upon so long, or pronounced with so much force as in the full accented syllables. But in the terminations *ice, ive, ile,* the vowel has generally its second sound, and the final *e* is superfluous, or only softens *c;* as notice, relative, juvenile,—pronounced notis, relativ, juvenil. In the former case, the final *e* is in Roman; and in the latter case, in Italic.

Di a phra*g*m	pleu ri sy	am or *ous*
du pli ca*te*	qui et u*de*	an ec dote
di a lo*gue*	*r*heu ma tism	an ti quate
aid de camp	ru min a*te*	ap ti tude
e go tism	scru pu lous	an o dyne
fa vor *ite*	se ri *ous*	ap er ture
for ci ble	spu ri *ous*	as y lum
fre quen cy	su i cide	bev e rage
fu *g*i tive	su*it* a ble	blun der buss
*s*e*a* si ble	va *ri ous*	cat a lo*gue*
glo ri *ous*	u ni form	cal cu late
he ro ism	u *s*u ry	can did ate
ju bi lee	*ă*d jec tive	can dle stick
ju ve ni*le*	ag gra va*te*	car a way
live li hood	an a pest	cel e brate
lu bri ca*te*	an im a*te*	crit i cism
lu cra tive	ap pe ti*te*	cim e tar
lu dic *rous*	al ti tude	court e sy
lu mi*n ous*	ab dic a*te*	cul tiv a*te*
ni*g*ht in ga*le*	ac cu rate	dec a lo*gue*
nu mer *ous*	ad e quate	dec o rate
o di *ous*	ac tu a*te*	ded ic a*te*
pre vi *ous*	ag o nize	def in *ite*
pa gan ism	al ge bra	del e gate

An Easy Standard of Pronunciation.

dem on strate	im pi ous	pen te cost
der o gate	in fa mous	per quis ite
des o late	in stig ate	phys ic al
des po tism	in sti tute	plen i tude
des pe rate	in tim ate	pres byt er
des ti tute	jeal ous y	pres id ent
dem a gogue	jeop ar dy	pris on er
ep au lette	jes sa mine	priv i lege
ep i logue	las si tude	quer u lous
el o quence	lat i tude	par a sol
el e vate	lib er tine	ral le ry
em pha sis	lit ig ate	ran cor ous
em u lous	mack er el	rap tur ous
en ter prize	mag ni tude	rav en ous
en vi ous	man u script	rec ti tude
ep i cure	mas sa cre	rel a tive
es tim ate	med i cine	ren o vate
ex cel lence	med it ate	re quis ite
fas cin ate	mis chiev ous	ren dez vous
fab u lous	met a phor	rep ro bate
feb ri fuge	musk mel on	res i dence
fluc tu ate	nour ish ment	res i due
fur be low	ped a gogue	ret i nue
gen er ous	pal li ate	rev er ence
gen tle man	pal pa ble	rev er end
gen u ine	pal pit ate	rhap so dy
grad u ate	par a ble	rhet o ric
gran a ry	par a dise	rid i cule
hem i sphere	par a digm	sac ri fice
hes it ate	par a phrase	sac ri lege
hand ker chief	par a site	sal iv ate
hur ri cane	par ent age	sas sa fras
hyp o crite	par ox ism	sat ir ize
im age ry	par ri cide	scav en ger

An Easy Standard of Pronunciation

sen si ble	lau da ble	crock e ry
sep a rate	plau si ble	hor i zon
ser a phim	por phy ry	lon gi tude
stadt hold er	arch i tect	nom in ate
stim u late	ar gu ment	ob lig ate
stip u late	ar ma ment	ob lo quy
stren u ous	ar ti fice	ob sta cle
sub ju gate	bay o net	ob stin ate
sub se quent	bar ba rism	ob vi ous
sub sti tute	bar ba rous	om in ous
syn a gogue	car din al	op e rate
sim i le	car pen ter	op po site
scep ti cism	chan cel lor	or i fice
syn co pe	chan ce ry	prob a ble
sur ro gate	guar di an	pop u lous
syc o phant	ghast li ness	pos i tive
syl lo gism	lar ce ny	pot en tate
tan ta lize	mar gin al	prof li gate
tan ta mount	mas quer ade	proph e cy
tel e scope	par ti san	quar an tine
ten a ble	phar ma cy	pros e cute
tim o rous	par lia ment	por rin ger
treach er ous	rasp ber ry	pros per ous
trip lic ate	al der man	pros ti tute
tur pi tude	al ma nac	sol e cism
vas sal age	bot a ny	sol i tude
vin dic ate	col lo quy	soph is try
bil let doux	com pli ment	vol a tile
fraud u lent	com plai sance	roq ue laur
cor di al	con sti tute	tom a hawk
cor po ral	con tem plate	per se cute
for feit ure	com pen sate	per son age
for ti tude	con fis cate	prin ci ple
for tu nate	cor o ner	serv i tude

An Easy Standard of Pronunciation.

ter min ate	com pa ny	roy al ty
firm a ment	come li ness	*ou*
mir a cle	gov ern or	coun sel lor
cir cu lar	gov ern ess	coun ter feit
cir cum stance	*oi*	coun te nance
cir cum spect	poig nan cy	boun ti ful

TABLE XX.

LESSON I.

MY son, hear the counsel of thy father, and forsake not the law of thy mother.

If sinners entice thee to sin, consent thou not.

Walk not in the way with them; refrain thy feet from their path, for their feet run to evil, and make haste to shed blood.

II.

Be not wise in thine own eyes, but be humble.

Let truth only proceed from thy mouth.—Despise not the poor, because he is poor; but honor him who is honest and just. Envy not the rich, but be content with thy fortune. Follow peace with all men, and let wisdom direct thy steps.

III.

Happy is the man that findeth wisdom. She is of more value than rubies. Length of days is in her right hand, and in her left hand riches and honor. Her ways are pleasant, and all her paths are peace. Exalt her and she shall promote thee: She shall bring thee to honor when thou dost embrace her.

IV.

The ways of virtue are pleasant, and lead to life, but they who hate wisdom, love death. Therefore pursue the paths of virtue and peace, then safety and glory will be thy reward. All my delight is upon the saints that are in the earth, and upon such as excel in virtue.

An Easy Standard of Pronunciation.

TABLE XXI.

Words of three syllables accented on the second.

A chiev ment	con jec ture	mis pris ion
ac quaint ance	con vuls ive	pneu mat ics
ap prais er	de ben ture	pre sump tive
ar rear age	de fect ive	pro duc tive
blas phe mer	dis cour age	pro gres sive
con ta gion	dis par age	re puls ive
con ta gious	dis sem ble	re ten tive
cor ro sive	ef ful gent	re venge ful
cour age ous	en tan gle	rheu mat ic
de ceit ful	ex cul pate	stu pend ous
de ci sive	gym nas tic	sub mis sive
dif fu sive	ef fect ive	ab or tive
in qui ry	em bez zle	in dorse ment
e gre gious	en deav or	im port ance
en light en	ex cess ive	im pos ture
o bei sance	ex pens ive	per form ance
out rage ous	ex press ive	re cord er
pro ce dure	ex tens ive	mis for tune
po ta toe	ex cheq uer	ad van tage
so no rous	es cutch eon	a part ment
mus ke toe	ho san na	de part ment
a bridge ment	il lus trate	dis as ter
ac knowl edge	i am bus	em bar go
ad ven ture	in cen tive	a pos tle
af fran chise	in cul cate	re mon strate
ag grand ize	in dent ure	sub al tern
dis fran chise	in jus tice	ac cou ter
ap pren tice	in vec tive	ma neu ver
au tum nal	lieu ten ant	al tern ate
bis sex tile	mo ment ous	de ter mine
com pul sive	of fens ive	re hears al
cur mud geon	op pres sive	sub vers ive

An Easy Standard of Pronunciation.

The following are accented on the first and third syllables.

Ap per tàin	con nois seur	em bra sure
ad ver tise	dis ap pear	ac qui esce
as cer tain	en ter tain	co a lesce
con tra vene	gaz et teer	male con tent
can non ade	deb o nair	coun ter mànd

TABLE XXII.

Words not exceeding three syllables, divided.

LESSON I.

THE wick-ed flee when no man pur-su-eth ; but the right-e-ous are as bold as a li-on.

Vir-tue ex-alt-eth a na-tion ; but sin is a re-proach to a-ny peo-ple.

The law of the wise is a foun-tain of life to de-part from the snares of death.

Wealth got-ten by de-ceit, is soon wast-ed ; but he that gath-er-eth by la-bor, shall in-crease in rich-es.

II.

I-dle-ness will bring thee to pov-er-ty ; but by in-dus-try and pru-dence thou shalt be fill-ed with bread.

Wealth mak-eth ma-ny friends ; but the poor are for-got-ten by their neigh-bors.

A pru-dent man fore-seeth the e-vil, and hid-eth him-self ; but the thought-less pass on and are pun-ish-ed.

III.

Train up a child in the way he should go ; and when he is old he will not de-part from it.

Where there is no wood the fire go-eth out, and where there is no tat-ler the strife ceas-eth.

A word fit-ly spok-en is like ap-ples of gold in pic-tures of sil-ver

An Easy Standard of Pronunciation.

He that cov-er-eth his sins shall not pros-per, but he that con-fess-eth and for-sak-eth them shall find mer-cy.

IV

The rod and re-proof give wis-dom ; but a child left to him-self bring-eth his pa-rents to shame.

Cor-rect thy son, and he will give thee rest ; yea, he will give thee de-light to thy soul.

A man's pride shall bring him low ; but hon-or shall up-hold the hum-ble in spir-it.

The eye that mock-eth at his fath-er, and scorn-eth to o-bey his moth-er, the ra-vens of the val-ley shall pick it out, and the young ea-gles shall eat it.

V.

By the bless-ing of the up-right, the cit-y is ex-alt-ed, but it is o-ver-thrown by the mouth of the wick-ed.

Where no coun-sel is, the peo-ple fall ; but in the midst of coun-sel-lors there is safe-ty.

The wis-dom of the pru-dent is to un-der-stand his way, but the fol-ly of fools is de-ceit.

A wise man fear-eth and de-part-eth from e-vil, but the fool ra-geth and is con-fi-dent.

Be not hast-y in thy spir-it to be an-gry ; for an-ger rest-eth in the bo-som of fools.

TABLE XXIII.

Words of four syllables, accented on the first.

2	des pi ca ble	mis er a ble
Ad mi ra ble	e li gi ble	nav i ga ble
ac cu rate ly	es ti ma ble	pal li a tive
am i ca ble	ex pli ca tive	pit i a ble
ap pli ca ble	fig u ra tive	pref er a ble
ar ro gant ly	lam ent a ble	ref er a ble
cred it a ble	lit er a ture	rev o ca ble
crim in al ly	mar riage a ble	sump tu ous ly

An Easy Standard of Pronunciation.

spec u la tive	à mi a ble	cŏm mon al ty
suf fer a ble	ju di ca ture	nom in a tive
tem per a ture	va ri a ble	op er a tive
val u a ble	hŏs pit a ble	prof it a ble
ven er a ble	for mid a ble	tol er a ble
vul ner a ble	ån swer a ble	cop u la tive

The following have the half accent on the third syllable

Ag ri cul ture	tab er na cle	årch i tect ure
an ti qua ry	tran sit o ry	ar bi tra ry
ap o plex y	åu dit o ry	par si mo ny

———

TABLE XXIV.

Words of four syllables; the full accent on the second, and half accent on the fourth.

Note. The terminations *ty*, *ry*, and *ly*, have very little accent.

Ad vi sa ble	im me di ate	vic to ri ous
ac cu mu late	im pe ri ous	vo lu min ous
ap pro pri ate	im pla ca ble	ux o ri ous
an ni hi late	in tu i tive	as pår a gus
a me na ble	la bo ri ous	ac cel er ate
ab bre vi ate	me lo di ous	ad mis si ble
al le vi ate	mys te ri ous	ad ven tur ous
cen so ri ous	no to ri ous	a dul ter ate
com mo di ous	ob se qui ous	ac cept a ble
com mu ni cate	op pro bri ous	ag gran dize ment
con cu pis cence	pe nu ri ous	dis fran chise ment
com pa ra ble	pre ca ri ous	am big u ous
de plo ra ble	sa lu bri ous	am phib i ous
dis pu ta ble	spon ta ne ous	a nal y sis
er ro ne ous	ter ra que ous	ar tic u late
har mo ni ous	vi ca ri ous	as sas sin ate

An Easy Standard of Pronunciation.

be at i tude	im pet u ous	e nor mi ty
ca lam ni ate	in dus tri ous	sub or din ate
ca pit u late	in gen u ous	a bom in ate
cer tif i cate	in quis i tive	ac com mo date
ca tas tro phe	in vid i ous	a non y mous
co ag u late	in vin ci ble	a poc a lypse
com bus ti ble	in vis i ble	a poc ry pha
com mem o rate	per fid i ous	a pos tro phe
com mis er ate	per spic u ous	cor rob o rate
com par a tive	pre dic a ment	de nom in ate
com pat i ble	per plex i ty	de mon stra ble
com pend i ous	pro mis cu ous	de pop u late
con grat u late	pa rish ion er	dis con so late
con spic u ous	re cep ta cle	pre pos ter ous
con tem pla tive	ri dic u lous	pre rog a tive
con tempt i ble	si mil i tude	re spons i ble
con tig u ous	sus cep ti ble	ad mis si ble
de fin i tive	tem pest u ous	con vers a ble
de lib er ate	tu mult u ous	re vers i ble
de riv a tive	vi cis si tude	su per flu ous
di min u tive	vo cif er ous	su per la tive
e phem e ris	vo lup tu ous	pre serv a tive
e piph a ny	u nan im ous	ac com pa ny
fa cil it ate	de bauch e ry	dis cov er y
fa nat i cism	con form i ty	*oi*
il lus tri ous	de form i ty	em broid er y

TABLE XXV.

THERE are five states of human life, infancy, child-hood, youth, manhood, and old age. The infant is help-less ; he is nourished with milk—when he has teeth, he begins to eat bread, meat, and fruit, and is very fond of

An Easy Standard of Pronunciation.

cakes and plums. The little boy chuses some plaything
that will make a noise, a hammer, a stick or a whip.
The little girl loves her doll and learns to dress it. She
chuses a closet for her baby-house, where she sets her
doll in a little chair, by the side of a table, furnished with
tea-cups as big as a thimble.

As soon as boys are large enough, they run away from
home, grow fond of play, climb trees to rob birds' nests,
tear their clothes, and when they come home, their pa-
rents often chastise them.—O how the rod makes their
legs smart. These are naughty boys, who love play better than their books—cruel boys, who rob the birds of
their eggs,—poor little birds which do no harm, which
fill the air with the sweet melody of their notes, and do
much good by devouring the worms, and other insects,
which destroy the fruits and herbage.

Charles, how many barley corns make an inch?
Three.—How many inches are in a foot? Twelve.—
How many feet in a yard? Three.—How many yards
in a rod, perch, or pole? Five and a half.—How many
rods in a mile? Three hundred and twenty.—How
many rods in a furlong? Forty.—How many furlongs
in a mile? Eight.—How many miles in a league?
Three.—How many lines in an inch? Twelve.—What
is a cubit? The length of the arm from the elbow to the
end of the longest finger, which is about eighteen inches.
A fathom is the distance of the ends of a man's fingers,
when the arms are extended, which is about six feet.

Henry, tell me the gills in a pint. Four. Two pints
make a quart, four quarts make a gallon. Barrels are of
various sizes ; some contain no more than twenty-seven
gallons, some thirty, or thirty-two, others thirty-six. A
hogshead contains sixty-three gallons ; but we usually
call puncheons by the name of hogsheads, and these
hold about one hundred and ten gallons. A pipe contains two hogsheads, or four barrels, or about one hundred and twenty gallons.

An Easy Standard of Pronunciation.

TABLE XXVI.

Words of five syllables; the full accent on the second.

Co têm po ra ry	pre par a to ry
de clam a to ry	pro hib it o ry
de fam a to ry	re sid u a ry
dis pen sa to ry	tu mul tu a ry
e lec tu a ry	vo cab u la ry
e pis to la ry	vo lup tu a ry
ex clam a to ry	con sòl a to ry
ex plan a to ry	de pos i to ry
ex tem po ra ry	de rog a to ry
he red it a ry	in vol un ta ry
in cen di a ry	re pos i to ry
in flam ma to ry	ob serv a to ry
pre lim i na ry	de lib er a tive
com mù ni ca ble	ef fem in a cy
com mu ni ca tive	in suf fer a ble
in vi o la ble	in dis so lu ble
per spi ra to ry	in vul ner a ble
de gén er a cy	in vet er a cy
con fed er a cy	in ter min a ble
con sid er a ble	in tem per ate ly

—

TABLE XXVII.

WILLIAM, tell me how many mills make a cent?
Ten.—How many cents a dime? Ten.—Tell me the
other coins of the United States. Ten dimes make a
dollar, ten dollars an eagle, which is a gold coin, and the
largest which is coined in the United States. Dimes

An Easy Standard of Pronunciation.

and dollars are silver coins.   Cents are copper coins.
These are new species of coin—What is the ancient
manner of reckoning money? By pounds, shillings,
pence, and farthings.   Four farthings make a penny,
twelve pence a shilling, and twenty shillings a pound.

William loves fruit.   See him picking strawberries—
bring him a basket—let him put the berries in a basket
and carry them to his mamma and sisters.   Little boys
should be kind and generous—they should always carry
some fruit home for their friends. Observe the cherry trees
—see how they begin to redden—in a few days, the cherries will be ripe ; the honey-hearts, the black-hearts,
and ox-hearts, how sweet they are. You must not eat too
many, and make yourself sick.   Fill your basket with
cherries, and give them to your little friends.

Now see the pears.   The harvest pear, how yellow.
It is ripe, let me pick and eat it.   The sugar pear, how
plump and soft it is , and what a beautiful red covers one
side of it.   See the catherine pear, and the vergaloo,
how rich, juicy, and delicious.   But the peach—how it
exceeds all fruit in its delicious flavor; what can equal
its fragrance, and how it melts upon the tongue.   The
nutmeg, the rare-ripe with its blushing cheek, the white
cling-stone with its crimson tints—and the lemon cling-
stone with its golden hue, and all the varieties of the
free-stones.   Such are the rich bounties of nature, bestowed on man to please his taste, preserve his health,
and draw his grateful heart towards the Author of his
happiness.

REMARKS.

A wise man will consider, not so much the present
pleasure and advantage of a measure, as its future con-
sequences.

Sudden and violent passions are seldom durable.

An Easy Standard of Pronunciation.

TABLE XXVIII.

Words of five syllables, accented on the first and third.

Am bi gu i ty	reg u lar i ty
con ti gu i ty	rep re hen si ble
con tra ri e ty	rep re sen ta tive
dic ta to ri al	sat is fac to ry
ep i cu re an	sen si bil i ty
im por tu ni ty	sen su al i ty
no to ri e ty	sim i lar i ty
op por tu ni ty	sin gu lar i ty
per pe tu i ty	tes ta ment a ry
per spi cu i ty	cir cum am bi ent
pres by te ri an	com pre hen si ble
pri mo ge ni al	con san guin i ty
su per flu i ty	con tra dict o ry
tes ti mo ni al	cred i bil i ty
aç a dem ic al	di a met ric al
af fa bil i ty	el e ment a ry
al pha bet ic al	ep i dem ic al
an a lyt ic al	e van gel ic al
ar gu ment a tive	fal li bil i ty
mon o syl la ble	gen e al o gy
plau si bil i ty	hos pi tal i ty
pol y syl la ble	il le git im ate
pop u lar i ty	im per cep ti ble
pos si bil i ty	in tel lect u al
pri mo gen i ture	in tro duc to ry
prin ci pal i ty	in tre pid i ty
prob a bil i ty	ir re sist i ble
prod i gal i ty	mag na nim i ty
punc tu al i ty	met a phys ic al
pu sil lan im ous	an a tom ic al

An Easy Standard of Pronunciation.

an i mos i ty	in ter rog a tive
a pos tol ic al	met a phor ic al
ar is toc ra cy	pe ri od ic al
as tro nom ic al	phi lo soph ic al
cat e gor ic al	phys i og no my
cu ri os i ty	phys i ol o gy
di a bol ic al	trig o nom e try
et y mol o gy	u ni form i ty
gen e ros i ty	u ni ver si ty
e qui pon der ant	em blem at ic al
in dis solv a ble	ge o graph ic al

TABLE XXIX.

Lesson I.

BE not anxious for your life, what ye shall eat, or what ye shall drink ; nor for your body, what ye shall put on ; for your heavenly Father knoweth that ye have need of these things.

Behold the fowls of the air : For they sow not, neither do they reap, nor gather into barns ; yet your heavenly Father feedeth them.

Consider the lilies of the field, how they grow ; they toil not, neither do they spin ; and yet Solomon in all his glory was not arrayed like one of these.

II.

Therefore be not anxious for the good things of this life, but seek first the kingdom of heaven and its righteousness, and all these things shall be added to you.

Ask, and it shall be given unto you : seek, and ye shall find : knock, and it shall be opened.

Love your enemies ; bless them that curse you ; do good unto them that hate you ; and pray for them that scornfully use you and persecute you.

An Easy Standard of Pronunciation.

III.

When thou prayest, be not as the hypocrites, who love to pray standing in the synagogues, and in the streets, that they may be seen of men : But when thou prayest, enter into thy closet, and when thou hast shut thy door, pray to thy Father who is in secret, and thy Father who seeth in secret shall reward thee openly.

IV.

Lay not up for yourselves treasures on earth, where moth and rust doth corrupt, and where thieves break through and steal : but lay up for yourselves treasures in heaven, where neither moth nor rust doth corrupt, and where thieves do not break through and steal : For where your treasure is, there will your heart be also.

Our Savior's Golden Rule.

ALL things which you would have men do to you, do ye the same to them ; for this is the law and the prophets.

TABLE XXX.

In the following words, *tion, tian, tial* and *tier*, are pronounced *chun, chal, chur.*

Côur tier	fus tian	com bus tion
bås tion	mix tion	di ges tion
christ ian	ce lês tial	ad mix tion

And in all words where *t* is preceded by *s* or *x.*

In all other words *tion* is pronounced *shun;* as are also *cion, cyon, sion.* Thus, *motion, coercion, halcyon, mansion,* are pronounced *moshun, coershun, halshun, manshun. Cial* is pronounced *shal.*

Words of two syllables accented on the first.

Mô tion	por tion	sta tion
na tion	po tion	ăc tion
no tion	ra tion	dic tion

An Easy Standard of Pronunciation.

fac tion	men tion	ses sion
fic tion	mis sion	ten sion
frac tion	pas sion	unc tion
fric tion	pen sion	auc tion
func tion	sanc tion	op tion
man sion	sec tion	ver sion

Words of three syllables accented on the second.

Ces sa tion	com mis sion	pro tec tion
com mo tion	com pres sion	pre emp tion
de vo tion	con fes sion	re demp tion
plant a tion	con sump tion	re flec tion
pol lu tion	con ven tion	sub jec tion
pro por tion	con vic tion	suc ces sion
re la tion	cor rec tion	sus pen sion
sal va tion	de cep tion	as per sion
fi du cial	de scrip tion	as ser tion
ad mis sion	di rec tion	a ver sion
af fec tion	dis tinc tion	con ver sion
af flic tion	ex cep tion	de ser tion
as cen sion	ex pres sion	dis per sion
as sump tion	in flic tion	re ver sion
at ten tion	ob jec tion	sub ver sion
col lec tion	pro fes sion	sub stan tial

Words of four syllables; the full accent on the third,
and the half accent on the first.

Ac cep ta tion	cal cu la tion
ac cu sa tion	con dem na tion
ad mi ra tion	con gre ga tion
ad o ra tion	con sti tu tion
ag gra va tion	con tem pla tion
ap pro ba tion	cul ti va tion
av o ca tion	dec la ra tion

An Easy Standard of Pronunciation.

des o la tion	res o lu tion
ed u ca tion	rev e la tion
el o cu tion	rev o lu tion
em u la tion	sep a ra tion
ex pect a tion	sup pli ca tion
hab it a tion	trib u la tion
in clin a tion	vi o la tion
in sti tu tion	vis it a tion
med it a tion	ap pre hen sion
mod e ra tion	com pre hen sion
nav i ga tion	con de scen sion
ob serv a tion	con tra dic tion
per se cu tion	ju ris dic tion
pres erv a tion	res ur rec tion
proc la ma tion	sat is fac tion
pub lic a tion	aug ment a tion
ref orm a tion	al ter a tion

Words of five syllables, accented on the first and fourth

Am pli fi ca tion	con fed e ra tion
qual i fi ca tion	con grat u la tion
ed i fi ca tion	con so ci a tion
as so ci a tion	or gan i za tion
mul ti pli ca tion	co op e ra tion
con tin u a tion	glo ri fi ca tion
rat i fi ca tion	pro nun ci a tion
sanc ti fi ca tion	pro pi ti a tion
sig ni fi ca tion	re gen e ra tion
cir cum lo cu tion	re nun ci a tion
cir cum val la tion	re tal i a tion
com mem o ra tion	ar gu ment a tion

Note. *As-sas-sin-a-tion, de-nom-in-a-tion, de-ter-min-a-tion, il-lu-min-a-tion,* have the second and fourth syllables accented, and *tran-sub-stan-ti-a-tion* has an accent on the first, third and fifth syllables. *Con-sub-stan-ti-a-tion* follows the same rule.

An Easy Standard of Pronunciation.

TABLE XXXI.

Familiar Lessons

HENRY is a good boy. Come here, Henry, let me hear you read. Can you spell easy words? Hold up your head; speak loud and plain. Keep your book clean; do not tear it.

John, keep your seat, and sit still. You must not say a word, nor laugh, nor play. Look on your book, learn your letters, study your lesson.

Charles, can you count? Try. One, two, three, four, five, six, seven, eight, nine, ten.—Well said; now spell bird. B-i-r-d. How the birds sing and hop from branch to branch among the trees They make nests too, and lay eggs; then sit on their eggs and hatch young birds. Dear little birds, how they sing and play. You must not rob their nests, nor kill their young: it is cruel.

Moses, see the cat, how quiet she lies by the fire. Puss catches mice. Did you ever see puss watching for mice? How still and sly! She creeps along, fixing her eyes steady on the place where the mouse lies. As soon as she gets near enough, she darts forward, and seizes the little victim by the neck. Now the little mouse will do no more mischief.

See the little helpless kittens. How warm and quiet they lie in their bed while puss is gone. Take them in your hands, don't hurt them; they are harmless, and do no hurt. They will not bite nor scratch. Lay them down softly, and let them go to sleep.

George, the sun has risen, and it is time for you to rise. See the sun, how it shines: it dispels the darkness of night, and makes all nature gay and cheerful. Get up, Charles; wash your hands, comb your hair, and get ready for breakfast. What are we to have for breakfast? Bread and milk. This is the best food

An Easy Standard of Pronunciation.

for little boys. Sometimes we have coffee or tea, and toast. Sometimes we have cakes.

James, hold your spoon in your right hand ; and if you use a knife and fork, hold the knife in your right hand. Do not eat fast : hungry boys are apt to eat fast, like the pigs. Never waste your bread ; bread is gained by the sweat of the brow. Your father plants or sows corn ; corn grows in the field ; when it is ripe, it is cut and put into the barn ; then it is thrashed out of the ears, and sent to a mill : the mill grinds it, and the bolter separates the bran from the flour. Flour is wet with water or milk ; and with a little yeast or leaven, it is raised, and made light ; this is called dough : dough is baked in an oven, or pan, and makes bread.

THE SISTERS

Emily, look at the flowers in the garden. What a charming sight. How the tulips adorn the borders of the alleys, dressing them with gaiety. Soon the sweet pinks will deck the beds ; and the fragrant roses perfume the air. Take care of the sweetwilliams, the jonquils, and the artemisia. See the honey-suckle, how it winds about the column, and climbs along the margin of the windows. Now it is in bloom, how fragrant the air around it ; how sweet the perfume, after a gentle shower, or amidst the soft dews of the evening. Such are the charms of youth, when robed in innocence ; such is the bloom of life, when decked with modesty, and a sweet temper.—Come, my child, let me hear your song.

The Rose

The rose had been wash'd, lately wash'd in a show'r,
  That Julia to Emma convey'd ;
A plentiful moisture encumber'd the flow'r,
  And weigh'd down its beautiful head.

An Easy Standard of Pronunciation.

The cup was all fill'd, and the leaves were all wet,
     And seem'd, at a fanciful view,
To weep with regret, for the buds it had left,
     On the flourishing bush where it grew.

I hastily seiz'd it, unfit as it was
     For a nosegay, so dripping and drown'd,
And shaking it rudely,—too rudely, alas,
     I snapt it—it fell to the ground.

" And such," I exclaim'd, " is the pitiless part
     " Some act by the delicate mind;
" Regardless of wringing and breaking a heart
     " Already to sorrow resign'd.

" This beautiful rose, had I shaken it less,
     " Might have bloom'd with the owner awhile;
" And tho tear that is wip'd with a little address,
     " May be follow'd perhaps by a smile."

Julia, rise in the morning betimes, dress the borders
of the flower beds, pull up the noxious weeds, water
the thirsty roots. See how the plants wither for want
of rain. The flowers fade, the leaves shrivel and droop.
Bring a little water to refresh them. Now the plants
look green and fresh; the weeds which shaded or robbed their roots of moisture, are removed, and the plants
will thrive. Does the heart want culture? Weed out
the noxious passions from the heart, as you would hurtful
plants from among the flowers. Cherish the virtues—
love, kindness, meekness, modesty, goodness. Let them
thrive, and produce their natural fruit, pure happiness,
and joys serene through life.

Look to the gentle lambs, how innocent and playful;
how agreeable to the sight; how pleasant the task to
feed them; how grateful they are for your care. Julia,
let me hear your song.

The Lamb.

A young feeble Lamb, as Emily pass'd,
     In pity she turn'd to behold;
How it shiver'd and shrunk from the merciless blast,
     Then fell all benumb'd with the cold.

An Easy Standard of Pronunciation.

She rais'd it, and touch'd with the innocent's fate,
    Its soft form to her bosom she prest;
But the tender relief was afforded too late,
    It bleated, and died on her breast.

The moralist then, as the corse she resign'd,
    And weeping, spring flow'rs o'er it laid,
Thus mus'd, " So it fares with the delicate mind,
    " To the tempest of fortune betray'd;

" Too tender, like thee, the rude shock to sustain,
    " And deni'd the relief which would save,
" She's lost, and when pity and kindness are vain,
    " Thus we dress the poor sufferer's grave."

Harriet, bring your book, let me hear you read.
What book have you? Let me see: a little volume of
poems. How many can you repeat? Let me hear my
dear Harriet speak one.

The Bird's Nest.

Yes, little nest, I'll hold you fast,
    And little birds, one, two, three, four;
I've watch'd you long, you're mine at last;
    Poor little things, you'll 'scape no more.

Chirp, cry, and flutter, as you will,
    Ah! simple rebels, 'tis in vain;
Your little wings are unfledg'd still,
    How can you freedom then obtain?

What note of sorrow strikes my ear;
    Is it their mother thus distrest?
Ah yes; and see, their father dear
    Flies round and round, to seek their nest.

And is it I who cause their moan?
    I, who so oft in summer's heat,
Beneath yon oak have laid me down
    To listen to their songs so sweet?

If from my tender mother's side
    Some wicked wretch should make me fly,
Full well I know, 'twould her betide,
    To break her heart, to sink, to die.

And shall I then so cruel prove,
    Your little ones to force away!
No; no; together live and love;
    See, here they are—take them I pray.

An Easy Standard of Pronunciation.

Teach them in yonder wood to fly,
    And let them your sweet warbling hear,
Till their own wings can soar as high,
    And their own notes may sound as clear.

Go, gentle birds; go free as air,
    While oft again, in summer's heat,
To yonder oak I will repair,
    And listen to your songs so sweet.

Mary, what a charming little sonnet your sister Harriet
has repeated. Come, my sweet girl, you must let me
hear what you can say. But stop, let me see your work.
Your little fingers are very handy with a needle. Very
pretty indeed, very pretty work. What small stitches.
You shall hem and mark all your papa's handkerchiefs,
and very soon you shall work a muslin frock for yourself. Now, my girl, let me hear you repeat some verses.

On a Goldfinch starved in his Cage.

Time was when I was free as air,
The thistle's downy seed my fare.
    My drink the morning dew:
I perch'd at will on every spray,
My form genteel, my plumage gay,
    My strains for ever new.

But gaudy plumage, sprightly strain,
And form genteel, were all in vain,
    And of a transient date;
For caught and cag'd, and starv'd to death,
In dying sighs my little breath
    Soon pass'd the wiry grate.

Thanks, little Miss, for all my woes,
And thanks for this effectual close,
    And cure of ev'ry ill;
More cruelty could none express,
And I, if you had shown me less,
    Had been your pris'ner still

An Easy Standard of Pronunciation.

Precepts concerning the Social Relations.

ART thou a young man, seeking for a partner for life? Obey the ordinance of God, and become a useful member of society. But be not in haste to marry, and let thy choice be directed by wisdom.

Is a woman devoted to dress and amusement? Is she delighted with her own praise, or an admirer of her own beauty? Is she given to much talking and loud laughter? If her feet abide not at home, and her eyes rove with boldness on the faces of men—turn thy feet from her, and suffer not thy heart to be ensnared by thy fancy.

But when thou findest sensibility of heart joined with softness of manners; an accomplished mind and religion, united with sweetness of temper, modest deportment, and a love of domestic life—Such is the woman who will divide the sorrows, and double the joys of thy life. Take her to thyself; she is worthy to be thy nearest friend, thy companion, the wife of thy bosom.

Art thou a young woman, wishing to know thy future destiny? Be cautious in listening to the addresses of men. Art thou pleased with smiles and flattering words? Remember that man often smiles and flatters most, when he would betray thee.

Listen to no soft persuasion, till a long acquaintance and a steady, respectful conduct, have given thee proof of the pure attachment and honorable views of thy lover. Is thy suitor addicted to low vices? is he profane? is he a gambler? a tipler? a spendthrift? a haunter of taverns? has he lived in idleness and pleasure? has he acquired a contempt for thy sex in vile company? and above all, is he a scoffer at religion?—Banish such a man from thy presence; his heart is false, and his hand would lead thee to wretchedness and ruin.

An Easy Standard of Pronunciation.

Art thou a husband ?   Treat thy wife with tenderness and respect ; reprove her faults with gentleness ; be faithful to her in love ; give up thy heart to her in confidence, and alleviate her cares.

Art thou a wife ?   Respect thy husband ; oppose him not unreasonably, but yield thy will to his, and thou shalt be blest with peace and concord ; study to make him respectable. as well for thine own sake as for his ; hide his faults ; be constant in thy love ; and devote thy time to the care and education of the dear pledges of thy love.

Art thou a parent ?   Teach thy children obedience ; teach them temperance, justice, diligence in useful occupations ; teach them science ; teach them the social virtues, and fortify thy precepts by thine own example ; above all, teach them religion.   Science and virtue will make them respectable in this life—religion and piety alone can secure to them happiness in the life to come.

Art thou a brother or a sister ?   Honor thy character by living in the bonds of affection with thy brethren.   Be kind ; be condescending.   Is thy brother in adversity, assist him ; if thy sister is in distress, administer to her necessities and alleviate her cares.

Art thou a son or a daughter ?   Be grateful to thy father, for he gave thee life : and to thy mother, for she sustained thee.   Piety in a child is sweeter than the incense of Persia, yea, more delicious than odors, wafted by western gales, from a field of Arabian spices.   Hear the words of thy father, for they are spoken for thy good ; give ear to the admonitions of thy mother, for they proceed from her tenderest love.   Honor their gray hairs, and support them in the evening of life ; and thine own children, in reverence of thy example, shall repay thy piety with filial love and duty.

An Easy Standard of Pronunciation.

FABLE I.

Of the Boy that stole Apples.

AN old Man found a rude Boy upon one of his trees stealing Apples, and desired him to come down ; but the young Sauce-box told him plainly he would not. Won't you? said the old Man, then I will fetch you down ; so he pulled up some tufts of Grass and threw at him ; but this only made the Youngster laugh, to think the old Man should pretend to beat him down from the tree with grass only.

Well, well, said the old Man, if neither words nor grass will do, I must try what virtue there is in stones : so the old Man pelted him heartily with stones, which soon made the young Chap hasten down from the tree and beg the old Man's pardon.

MORAL

If good words and gentle means will not reclaim the wicked, they must be dealt with in a more severe manner.

An Easy Standard of Pronunciation.

TABLE XXXII.

In all words ending in *ow* unaccented, *w* is silent, and *o* has its
first sound. Many of these words are corrupted in vulgar pronunciation; *follow* is called *foller*, &c. for which reason the
words of this class are collected in the following table.

Bår row	gal lows	nar row	win dow
bel low	bel lows	hol low	win now
bil low	har row	shad ow	yel low
bur row	cal low	shal low	bôr row
el bow	mal lows	spar row	fol low
fel low	mar row	tal low	môr row
fal low	mead ow	whit low	sor row
far row	mel low	wid ow	wal low
fur row	min now	wil low	swal low

TABLE XXXIII.

In the following words, *si* sounds like *zh*. Thus, *confu-sion* is
pronounced *confu-zhun; bra-sier, bra-zhur; o-sier, o-zhur;
vi-sion, vizh-un; pleas-ure, pleazh-ur.*

Note. In this and the following table, the figures show the accented syllables, without any other direction.

Brå sier	con fu sion	il lu sion
cro sier	con tu sion	in tru sion
gla zier	de lu sion	in fu sion
o sier	dif fu sion	pro fu sion
ra sure	ef fu sion	oc ca sion
ho sier	ex clu sion	ob tru sion
sei zure	ex plo sion	vîs ion
fu sion	e va sion	meas ure
am brô sial	a bra sion	pleas ure
ad he sion	cor ro sion	treas ure
al lu sion	de tru sion	leis ure
cô he sion	dis plo sion	az ure
col lu sion	in clo sure	ab scîs ion
con clu sion	e ro sion	col lis ion

An Easy Standard of Pronunciation.

con cis ion	e lis ion	in cis ion
di vis ion	e lys ian	al lis ion
de cis ion	pre cis ion	re cis ion
de ris ion	pro vis ion	cir cum cis ion

The compounds and derivatives follow the same rule.

FABLE II.

The Country Maid and her Milk pail.

WHEN men suffer their imagination to amuse them, with the prospect of distant and uncertain improvements of their condition, they frequently sustain real losses, by their inattention to those affairs in which they are immediately concerned.

A Country Maid was walking very deliberately with a pail of milk upon her head, when she fell into the following train of reflections : The money for which I shall sell this milk, will enable me to increase my stock of eggs to three hundred. These eggs, allowing for what may prove addle, and what may be destroyed by vermin, will produce at least two hundred and fifty chickens. The chickens will be fit to carry to

An Easy Standard of Pronunciation.

market about Christmas, when poultry always bears a
good price; so that by May day I cannot fail of having
money enough to purchase a new gown.   Green—let
me consider—yes, green becomes my complexion best,
and green it shall be.   In this dress I will go to the fair,
where all the young fellows will strive to have me for a
partner ; but I shall perhaps refuse every one of them,
and with an air of disdain, toss from them.   Transported
with this triumphant thought, she could not forbear acting with her head what thus passed in her imagination,
when down came the pail of milk, and with it all her
imaginary happiness.

———

TABLE XXXIV.

Words in which *cie*, *sie*, and *tie*, are pronounced *she; tia*, and *eia*,
sha; cious, and *tious*, *shus*.   Thus, *ancient*, *partial*, *captious*, are
pronounced, *anshent*, *parshal*, *capshus*.   This rule will be sufficient to direct the learner to a right pronunciation, without
distinguishing the silent letters.

Grè cian	tran sient	ex pa tiate
gra cious	lus cious	fa ce tious
pa tient	cầu tious	fal la cious
quo tient	pầr tial	fe ro cious
spa cious	cồn science	in gra tiate
spe cious	con scious	lo qua cious
spe cies*	ap prè ciate	ne go ciate
so cial	as so ciate	pro ca cious
sa tiate	au da cious	ra pa cious
ân cient	ca pa cious	sa ga cious
cap tious	con so ciate	se qua cious
fac tious	dis so ciate	te na cious
fic tious	e ma ciate	vex a tious
nup tial	ex cru ciate	vi va cious

* Pronounced *speshiz.*

An Easy Standard of Pronunciation.

vo ra cious	pro vin cial	cir cum stån tial
an nůn ciate	pru den tial	con sci en tious
con ten tious	sen ten tious	con se quen tial
cre den tials	sub stan tiate	con fi den tial
e nu, ciate	com mer cial	pen i ten tial
es sen tial	con tu mà cious†	pes ti len tial
in fec tious	ef fi ca cious	prov i den tial
li cen tiate	os ten ta tious	rev e ren tial
om nis cience	per spi ca cious	res i den tia ry
po ten tial	per ti na cious	e qui nòc tial

The compounds and derivatives follow the same rule.
† The words of four syllables have the half accent on the first.

FABLE III.

The Fox and the Swallow.

ARISTOTLE informs us, that the following fable was spoken by Esop to the Samians, on a debate upon changing their ministers, who were accused of plundering the commonwealth.

A Fox swimming across a river, happened to be entangled in some weeds that grew near the bank, from which

An Easy Standard of Pronunciation.

he was unable to extricate himself.   As he lay thus exposed to whole swarms of flies, which were galling him
and sucking his blood, a swallow observing his distress,
kindly offered to drive them away.   By no means, said
the Fox; for if these should be chased away, which are
already sufficiently gorged, another more hungry swarm
would succeed, and I should be robbed of every remain-
ing drop of blood in my veins.

TABLE XXXV.

In the following words the vowels are short, and the accented
syllables must be pronounced as though it ended with the consonants *sh*. Thus *pre-cious*, *spe-cial*, *effi-cient*, *logi-cian*, *mili-tia*,
addi-tion, are pronounced, *presh-us*, *spesh-ul*, *effish-ent*, *logish-*
an, *milish-a*, *addish-on*. These words will serve as examples
for the following table.

Prē cious	ef fi cient	per di tion
spe cial	es pe cial	per ni cious
vi cious	fla gi tious	pe ti tion
vi tiate	fru i tion	pro fi cient
ad di tion	ju di cial	phy si cian
am bi tion	lo gi cian	po si tion
aus pi cious	ma gi cian	pro pi tious
ca pri cious	ma li cious	se di tion
co mi tial	mi li tia	se di tious
con di tion	mu si cian	sol sti tial
cog ni tion	nu tri tion	suf fi cient
con tri tion	no vi ciate	sus pi cious
de fi cient	of fi ciate	trans i tion
de li cious	of fi cial	vo li tion
dis cre tion	of fi cious	ab o li tion*
dis cu tient	pa tri cian	ac qui si tion
e di tion	par ti tion	ad mo ni tion

* The words of four syllables have a half accent on the first,
except *practitioner*. *Arithmetician* and *supposititious* have the half
accent on the second, *academician* and *mathematician* on the first.

An Easy Standard of Pronunciation,

ad ven ti tious	prej u di cial	co a li tion
am mu ni tion	pol i ti cian	com pe ti tion
ap pa ri tion	prop o si tion	com po si tion
ar ti fi cial	prep o si tion	def i ni tion
ad sci ti tious	pro hi bi tion	dem o li tion
ap po si tion	*r*het o ri cian	dep o si tion
eb ul li tion	su per fi cial	dis po si tion
er u di tion	su per sti tion	prac ti tion er
ex hi bi tion	sup po si tion	a rith me ti cian
ex po si tion	sur rep ti tious	ac a de mi cian
im po si tion	av a ri cious	sup þos i ti tious
op po si tion	ben e fi cial	math e ma ti cian

The compounds and derivatives follow the same rule.

———◆———

In the following words, the consonant *q* terminates a syllable, but perhaps the ease of the learner may render a different division more eligible.

2	li q*u*or	an ti qui ty
E qui ty	li que fy	in i qui ty
e qui ta ble	li qui date	in i qui tous
li quid	la q*u*ey	ob li qui ty

SELECT SENTENCES.

Never speak of a man's virtues to his face, nor of his faults behind his back ; thus you will equally avoid flattery which is disgusting, and slander which is criminal.

If you are poor, labor will procure you food and clothing—if you are rich, it will strengthen the body, invigorate the mind, and keep you from vice.—Every man, therefore, should be busy in some employment.

An Easy Standard of Pronunciation.

FABLE IV.

The Cat and the Rat.

A CERTAIN Cat had made such unmerciful havoc among the vermin of her neighborhood, that not a single Rat nor Mouse ventured to appear abroad. Puss was soon convinced, that if affairs remained in their present situation, she must be totally unsupplied with provision. After mature deliberation, therefore, she resolved to have recourse to stratagem. For this purpose, she suspended herself from a hook with her head downwards, pretending to be dead. The Rats and Mice, as they peeped from their holes, observing her in this dangling attitude, concluded she was hanging for some misdemeanor; and with great joy immediately sallied forth in quest of their prey. Puss, as soon as a sufficient number were collected together, quitting her hold, dropped into the midst of them; and very few had the fortune to make good their retreat. This artifice having succeeded so well, she was encouraged to try the event of a second. Accordingly she whitened her coat all over, by rolling herself in a

An Easy Standard of Pronunciation.

heap of flour, and in this disguise lay concealed in the bottom of a meal tub. This stratagem was executed in general with the same effect as the former. But an old experienced rat, altogether as cunning as his adversary, was not so easily ensnared. I don't much like, said he, that white heap yonder; something whispers me there is mischief concealed under it. 'Tis true it may be meal, but it may likewise be something that I should not relish quite so well. There can be no harm at least in keeping at a proper distance; for caution, I am sure, is the parent of safety.

TABLE XXXVI.

In the follqwing table, *i* before a vowel sounds like *y* at the beginning of words, as in *junior, filial, dominion*, which are pronounced, *junyur, filyal, dominyun*.

Fŏl io	mill ion	in gen ious
jun ior	min ion	bat tăl ion
sol dier*	pill ion	ci vil ian
sav ior	pin ion	com pan ion
seign ior	trill ion	con nex ion
un ion	trunn ion	de flux ion
al ien	val iant	do min ion
gen ial	cull ion	fa mil iar
gen ius	runn ion	o pin ion
anx ious†	scull ion	pa vil ion
bdell ium	bull ion	post ill ion
bil ious	coll ier	punc till io
bill iards	pon iard	ras cal ion
bill ions	on ion	re bell ion
brill iant	be hav iour	se rag'l io
bagn io	com mun ion	ver mill ion
fil ial	par hel ion	aux il ia ry
fl n	pe cul iar	min ia ture
flux ion	con ven ient	pe căn ia ry

* Pronounced sol-ger.   † Pronounced ank-shus.

An Easy Standard of Pronunciation.

FABLE V

The Fox and the Bramble.

A FOX, closely pursued by a pack of Dogs, took
shelter under the covert of a Bramble.   He rejoiced in
this asylum ; and, for a while, was very happy ; but soon
found that if he attempted to stir, he was wounded by
thorns and prickles on every side.   However, making a
virtue of necessity, he forebore to complain ; and com-
forted himself with reflecting that no bliss is perfect ;
that good and evil are mixed, and flow from the same
fountain.   These Briars, indeed, said he, will tear my
skin a little, yet they keep off the dogs.   For the sake
of the good, then, let me bear the evil with patience ;
each bitter has its sweet ; and these Brambles, the
they wound my flesh, preserve my life from danger

An Easy Standard of Pronunciation.

TABLE XXXVII.

The first sound of *th*, as in *think*.

1		
E ther	the o rem	ca thăr tic
ja cinth	the a ter	en thŭ si asm
the sis	hy a cinth	an tĭp a thy
ze nith	căth o lic	pa renth e sis
thŭn der	ep i thet	a rith me tic
meth od	lab y rinth	an tith e sis
an them	leth ar gy	mis an thro py
dip thong	pleth o ry	phi lan thro py
eth ics	sym pa thy	can thar i des
pan ther	am a ranth	the ŏc ra cy
sab bath	am e thyst	the ol o gy
thim ble	ap a thy	the od o lite
this tle	can the rus	ther mom e ter
thurs day	math e sis	au thor i ty
trip thong	syn the sis	ca thol i con
en thrăl	pan the on	my thol o gy
ath wart	e thê ri al	or thog ra phy
be troth	can tha ris	hy poth e sis
thĭr ty	ca the dral	li thog ra phy
thor *ough*	u re thra	li thot o my
thir têen	au thĕn tic	a poth e ca ry
ou	pa thet ic	ap o thê o sis
thou sand	syn thet ic	pol y the ism
ᶑ the ism	a canth us	bib li o thê cal
the o ry	ath let ic	ich thy ŏl o gy
	me theg lin	or ni thol o gy

Second sound of *th*, as in *thou.*

êi ther	răth er	hith er	wea*th* er
nei ther	fath om	leath er	with er
hea then	fea*th* er	fur ther	wheth er
cloth ier	gath er	breth ren	neth er

An Easy Standard of Pronunciation.

weth er	whith er	brŏth er	be queath
prith ee	fȧ ther	wor thy	an ŏth er
bur then	far thing	moth er	to gĕth er
south ern	far ther	smoth er	lŏg a rithm*s*
teth er	pŏth er	oth er	nĕv er the l**ė**ss
thith er	broth el	be nĕath	

The derivatives follow the same rule.

FABLE VI.

The Bear and the Two Friends.

TWO Friends, setting out together upon a journey,
which led through a dangerous forest, mutually promised to assist each other, if they should happen to be as-
saulted.   They had not proceeded far, before they perceived a Bear making towards them with great rage.

There were no hopes in flight ; but one of them, being
very active, sprung up into a tree ; upon which the other, throwing himself flat on the ground, held his breath
and pretended to be dead ; remembering to have heard
it asserted, that this creature will not prey upon a dead
carcass.   The bear came up, and after smelling to him

An Easy Standard of Pronunciation.

some time, left him, and went on.—When he was fairly out of sight and hearing, the hero from the tree called out—Well, my friend, what said the bear? he seemed to whisper you very closely. He did so, replied the other, and gave me this good piece of advice, never to associate with a wretch, who in the hour of danger will desert his friend.

TABLE XXXVIII.

Words in which *ch* have the sound of *k*.

Christ	cŏl ic	or ches ter
chyle	chol er	och i my
scheme	schol ar	chi mĕ ra
ache	mon arch	pa ro chi al
chăsm	schîr rous	cha mel ion
chrism	stŏm ach	tri băc chus
chŏrd	pă tri arch	chro mat ic
loch	eu cha rĭst	me chan ic
schŏol	ăn ar chy	ca chex y
or	chrys o lite	cha lib e ate
choir	char ac ter	a nach ro nĭsm
chŏ rus	cat e chĭsm	syn ec do che
te trarch	pen ta teuch	pyr *r*hich i us
cha os	sep ul cher	am phib ri chus
cho ral	tech nic al	mĕl an chol y
e poch	al chy my	chro nŏl o gy
o cher	an cho ret	chi rog ra phy
tro chee	brach i al	cho rog ra phy
ăn· chor	lach ry mal	cĥro nom e ter
christ *e*n	mach in ate	the om a chy
chem ist	sac char ine	an ti băc chus
ech o	syn chro nĭsm	căt e chĕt ic al
chal ice	mich ael mas	Lac chan ăl ian
sched ule	chŏr is ter	cat e chu men
pas chal	chron i cle	ich thy ŏl o gy

An Easy Standard of Pronunciation.

FABLE VII.
The Two Dogs.

HASTY and inconsiderate connections are generally attended with great disadvantages ; and much of every man's good or ill fortune, depends upon the choice he makes of his friends.

A good-natured Spaniel overtook a surly Mastiff, as he was travelling upon the high road. Tray, although an entire stranger to Tiger, very civilly accosted him ; and if it would be no interruption, he said, he should be glad to bear him company on his way. Tiger, who happened not to be altogether in so growling a mood as usual, accepted the proposal ; and they very amicably pursued their journey together. In the midst of their conversation, they arrived at the next village, where Tiger began to display his malignant disposition, by an unprovoked attack upon every dog he met. The villagers immediately sallied forth with great indignation, to rescue their respective favorites ; and falling upon our two friends, without distinction or mercy, poor Tray was most cruelly treated, for no other reason but his being found in bad company

An Easy Standard of Pronunciation.

TABLE XXXIX.

Words of French original, in which *ch* sound like *sh*, and *i* accented like *e* long.

Châise	fa tigue	mag a zine
châm ois*	in trigue	bom ba sin
chan cre	ma rine	man da rin
cham âde	der nier	brig a dier
cham paign	po lice	bom oard ier
fra cheur	ma chine ry	buc can ier
chi cane	chev er il	can non ier
10	chev is ance	cap a pie
pique	chiv al ry	car bin ier
shire	deb au chee	cav a lier
10	10	cor de lier
ma chine	chev a lier	gren a dier
cash ier	chan de lier	fi nan cier
an tique	cap u chin	

* Pronounced shammy.

SELECT SENTENCES.

We may as well expect that God will make us rich without industry, as that he will make us good and happy without our own endeavors.

Zeno, hearing a young man very loquacious, told him, that men have two ears and but one tongue ; therefore they should hear much and speak little.

A man who, in company, engrosses the whole conversation, always gives offence ; for the company consider him as assuming a degree of superiority, and treating them all as his pupils.

The basis of all excellence in writing and conversation, is truth—truth is intellectual gold, which is as durable as it is splendid and valuable.

Faction seldom leaves a man honest, however it may find him.

An Easy Standard of Pronunciation.

FABLE VIII.

The partial Judge

A FARMER came to a neighboring Lawyer, expressing great concern for an accident which he said had just happened. One of your Oxen, continued he, has been gored by an unlucky Bull of mine, and I should be glad to know how I am to make you reparation. Thou art a very honest fellow, replied the Lawyer, and wilt not think it unreasonable that I expect one of thy Oxen in return. It is no more than justice, quoth the Farmer, to be sure ; but what did I say ?—I mistake— It is *your* Bull that has killed one of *my* Oxen. Indeed! says the Lawyer, that alters the case : I must inquire into the affair ; and if—And *if!* said the Farmer, the business I find would have been concluded without an *if*, had you been as ready to do justice to others as to exact it from them.

An Easy Standard of Pronunciation.

TABLE XL.

Words in which *g* is hard before *e, i,* and *y.*

Gĕar	dag ger	leg ged	g*h*erk in
geese	crag gy	pig gin	åu ger
gĕld	bug gy	quag gy	bŏg gy
get	crag ged	rag ged	fog gy
gift	dig ger	rig ger	clog gy
give	dreg gy	rig gish	cog ger
gig	drug get	rug ged	dog ged
gild	drug gist	scrag ged	dog ger
gill	flag gy	scrag gy	dog gish
gimp	gib ber	shag gy	jog ger
gĭrd	gib bous	slug gish	nog gen
girt	gid dy	snag ged	pår get
girl	gig gle	sprig gy	tar get
ĕa ger	gig let	stag ger	gĭr dle
mea ger	giz zard	swag ger	be gĭn
gew gaw	gim blet	swag gy	wäg ge ry
ti ger	hag gish	trig ger	lŏg ger head
to ged	jag gy	twig gin	or gĭl lous
bĭg gin	jag ged	twig gy	to geth er
brag ger	knag gy	wag gish	pĕt ti fŏg ger

The following are pronounced as though they were written with double *g.* Thus, *finger* is pronounced *fingger.*

Fĭn ger	lin ger	young er	long est
an ger	lin go	young est	strong er
hun ger	lin guist	long er	mŏng er

These, with their compounds and derivatives, are most of the words in the language, in which *g* has its hard sound before *e, i,* and *y.* But to these must be added the derivatives of verbs ending in *g.* Thus from *dig* come *diggeth, diggest, digged, digging,* &c. in which *g* is hard before *e* and *i.*

An Easy Standard of Pronunciation.

TABLE XLI.

*The Boy that went to the Wood to look for Birds' Nests,
when he should have gone to School.*

WHEN Jack got up, and put on his clothes, he
thought if he could get to the wood, he should be quite
well ; for he thought more of a bird's nest, than his
book, that would make him wise and great. When he
came there, he could find no nest, but one that was on
the top of a tree, and with much ado he got up to it, and
robbed it of the eggs.—Then he tried to get down ; but
a branch of the tree found a hole in the skirt of his coat,
and held him fast. At this time he would have been
glad to be at school ; for the bird, in a rage at the loss of
her eggs, flew at him, and was like to pick out his eyes.
Now it was that the sight of a man at the foot of the
tree, gave him more joy than all the nests in the world.
This man was so kind as to chase away the bird, and
help him down from the tree ; and from that time forth
he would not loiter from school ; but grew a good boy
and a wise young man, and had the praise and good
will of all that knew him.

OBSERVATIONS.

The cheerful man hears the lark in the morning , the
pensive man hears the nightingale in the evening.

He who desires no virtue in a companion, has no virtue himself ; and that state is hastening to ruin, in
which no difference is made between good and bad
men.

Some men read for the purpose of learning to write ;
others for the purpose of learning to talk ;—the former
study for the sake of science ; the latter, for the sake of
amusement.

An Easy Standard of Pronunciation.

TABLE XLII.

It is a rule in the language, that *c* and *g* are hard at the end of words, and they commonly are so at the end of syllables; but in the following table they are soft, like *s* and *j* at the end of the accented syllables. Thus, *magic, acid,* are pronounced *majic, asid,* and ought to be divided mag-ic, ac-id. It is a matter disputed by teachers which is the most eligible division—*mag-ic, ac-id,* or *ma-gic, a-cid.* However, as children acquire a habit of pronouncing *c* and *g* hard at the end of syllables, I choose not to break the practice, but have joined these consonants to the last syllable. The figures show that the vowels of the accented syllables are all short.

Mǎ gic	pa ci fy	ex pli cit
tra gic	pa geant ry	so li cit
a gile	pa gin al	im a gine
a cid	re gi cide	re li gion
di git	re gim en	li ti gious
vi gil	re gim ent	pro di gious
fa cile	re gis ter	au da ci ty
fra gile	spe ci fy	ca pa ci ty
fri gid	spe cim en	fu ga ci ty
ri gid	ma cer ate	lo qua ci ty
pla cid	ma cil ent	men da ci ty
pi geon	ma gis trate	men di ci ty
si gil	ne ces sa ry	di la cer ate
ta cit	tra ge dy	du pli ci ty
a git ate	vi cin age	fe li ci ty
ag ger ate*	ve get ate	mu ni ci pal
le gi ble	ve get ant	an ti ci pate
fla gel et	lo gic	par ti ci pate
pre ce dent	pro cess	sim pli ci ty
pre ci pice	co git ate	me di cin al
re ci pe	pro ge ny	so li ci tude
de cim al	il li cit	per ni ci ty
de cim ate	im pli cit	tri pli ci ty
la cer ate	e li cit	ver ti ci ty

* g soft.

An Easy Standard of Pronunciation.

au da ci ty	om ni gin ous	per spi ca ci ty
ex ag ger ate	ver ti gin ous	per ti na ci ty
mor da ci ty	re fri ger ate	a tró ci ty
nu ga ci ty	lè gis là tion	fe ro ci ty
o pa ci ty	re cit a tion	ve lo ci ty
ra pa ci ty	sa cri lẻ gious	rhi no ce ros
sa ga ci ty	o le a gin ous	an a lò gic al
se qua ci ty	au then ti ci ty	as tro lo gic al
vi va ci ty	e las ti ci ty	ge o lo gic al
te na ci ty	e lec tri ci ty	ped a go gic al
ve ra ci ty	du o de ci mo	phi lo lo gic al
a da gi o	ab o ri gin al	tau to lo gic al
bel li ger ent	ec cen tri ci ty	the o lo gic al
or i gin al	mu cil a gin ous	re ci pro ci ty
ar mi ger'ous	mul ti pli ci ty	lè ger de màin

The compounds and derivatives follow the same rule.

TABLE XLIII.

Words in which *h* is pronounced before *w*, though written after it. Thus, *what*, *when*, *whisper*, are pronounced *hwat*, *hwen*, *hwisper*; that is, *hooat*, *hooen*, *hooisper*.

Whåle	whelm	whit	wher ry
wheal	when	whiz	wheth er
wheat	whence	whurr	whif fle
wheel	whet	whårf	whim sey
wheeze	which	whåt	whin ny
while	whiff	whirl	whis per
whilst	whig	where	whis tle
whine	whim	whey	whith' er
white	whin	whee dle	whit low
why	whip	whi ting	whit ster
whelk	whisk	whi tish	whit tle
whelp	whist	wher ret	whim per

The compounds and derivatives follow the same rule.

In the following, with their compounds and derivatives, *w* is silent.

Whòre   whole   who   whom   whoop   whose

An Easy Standard of Pronunciation.

TABLE XLIV.

In the following, with their compounds and derivatives, *x* is pronounced like *gz; exact* is pronounced *egzact,* &c.

Ex åct	ex em pli fy	ex or bit ant
ex ist	ex an i mate	ex or di um
ex em*pt*	ex as pe rate	ex ålt
ex ult	ex úde	ex ot ic
ex am in*e*	ex a men	ex on er ate
ex am pl*e*	ex u ber anc*e*	ex ĕrt
ex em plar	ex håust	ex er cent
ex ec u tor	ex *h*ort	ĕx ile

In most or all other words, *x* is pronounced like *ks,* except at the beginning of Greek names, where it sounds like *z.*

TABLE XLV.

The History of the Creation of the World.

IN six days God made the world, and all things that are in it. He made the Sun to shine by day, and the Moon to give light by night.—He made all the beasts that walk on the earth, all the birds that fly in the air, and all the fish that swim in the sea. Each herb, and plant, and tree is the work of his hands. All things, both great and small, that live and move, and breathe in this wide world, to him do owe their birth, to him their life. And God saw that all the things he had made were good. But as yet there was not a man to till the ground ; so God made man of the dust of the earth, and breathed into him the breath of life, and gave him rule over all that he had made. And the man gave names to all the beasts of the field, the fowls of the air, and the fish of the sea. But there was not found an help meet for man ; so God brought on him a deep sleep, and then took from his side a rib, of which he made a wife, and

---

An Easy Standard of Pronunciation

gave her to the man, and her name was Eve—And from these two came all the sons of men.

All things are known to God ; though his throne of state is far on high, yet doth his eye look down upon us in this lower world, and see all the ways of the sons of men.

If we go out, he marks our steps : and when we go in, no door can shut him from us. While we are by ourselves, he knows all our vain thoughts, and the ends we aim at : And when we talk to friend or foe, he hears our words, and views the good or harm we do to them, or to ourselves.

When we pray, he notes our zeal. All the day long he minds how we spend our time, and no dark night can hide our works from him. If we play the cheat, he marks the fraud, and hears the least word of a false tongue.

He sees if our hearts are hard to the poor, or if by alms we help their wants : If in our breast we pine at the rich, or if we are well pleased with our own state. He knows all that we do ; and be we where we will, he is sure to be with us.

TABLE XLVI.

Examples of the formation of derivatives and compound words.

EXAMPLE I.

Words in which *or* or *er* are added to denote an agent.

Prim.	Deriv.	Prim.	Deriv.
Act,	act-or	in-struct,	in-struct-or
lead,	lead-er	blas-pheme,	blas-phe-mer
deal	deal-er	cor-rect,	cor-rect-or
gain,	gain-er	dis-pose,	dis-po-ser
hate,	ha-ter	op-press,	op-press-or
cool,	cool-er	re-deem,	re-deem-er
help,	help-er	dis-sent,	dis-sent-er

An Easy Standard of Pronunciation.

EXAMPLE II

Words to express females, or the feminine gender, formed from those which express males, or the masculine gender.

act-or,	act-ress	peer	peer-ess
bar-on,	bar-on-ess	priest.	priest-ess
tu-tor,	tu-tor-ess	prince,	prin-cess
trait-or,	trait-ress	po-et,	po-et-ess
count,	count-ess	song-ster,	song-stress
dea-con,	dea-con-ess	li-on,	li-on-ess
duke,	duch-ess	mas-ter,	mis-tress
heir,	heir-ess	em-pe-ror,	em-press
proph-et,	proph-et-ess	tes-ta-tor,	test-a-trix
sor-cer-er,	sor-cer-ess	seam-ster,	seam-stress

a-dul-ter-er,	a-dul-ter-ess
em-bas-sa-dor,	em-bas-sa-dress
shep-herd,	shep-herd-ess
ben-e-fac-tor,	ben-e-fac-tress
gov-ern-or,	gov-ern-ess
mar-quis,	mar-chi-o-ness
pro-tect-or	pro-tect-ress
ex-ec-u-tor,	ex-ec-u-trix
ad-min-is-tra-tor,	ad-min-is-tra-trix

EXAMPLE III.

Words formed by *ly*, (which is a contraction of *like*) used to denote a quality or show the manner of action, or degree of quality.

bad,	bad-ly	ab-struse,	ab-struse-ly
brave,	brave-ly	cow-ard,	cow-ard-ly
chief,	chief-ly	crook-ed,	crook-ed-ly
dark,	dark-ly	ex-act,	ex-act-ly
good,	good-ly	ef-fect-u-al,	ef-fect-u-al-ly
high,	high-ly	ex-cess-ive,	ex-cess-ive-ly
weak,	weak-ly	fa-ther,	fa-ther-ly
year,	year-ly	gal-lant,	gal-lant-ly
new,	new-ly	se-date,	se-date-ly

An Easy Standard of Pronunciation.

EXAMPLE IV.

Words formed by *ful*, denoting abundance.

mer-cy,	mer-ci-ful	de-ceit,	de-ceit-ful
mourn,	mourn-ful	re-spect,	re-spect-ful
hope,	hope-ful	dis-grace,	dis-grace-ful
wish,	wish-ful	de-light,	de-light-ful
youth,	youth-ful	re-venge,	re-venge-ful
awe,	aw-ful	dis-trust,	dis-trust-ful
care,	care-ful	du-ty,	du-ti-ful

EXAMPLE V.

Words formed by *able*, or *ible*, denoting power or ability.

com-mend,	com-mend-a-ble	cure,	cu-ra-ble
as-sail,	as-sail-a-ble	pay,	pay-a-ble
re-spire,	re-spi-ra-ble	sale,	sale-a-ble
per-spire,	per-spi-ra-ble	vend,	vend-i-ble
ad-vise,	ad-vi-sa-ble	test,	test-a-ble
re-verse,	re-vers-i-ble	taste,	tast-a-ble
man-age,	man-age-a-ble	tax,	tax-a-ble
cred-it,	cred-it-a-ble	tame,	tame-a-ble
prof-it,	prof-it-a-ble	rate,	rate-a-ble

EXAMPLE VI.

Words formed by *ness*, denoting a state or condition.

good,	good-ness	shrewd,	shrewd-ness
great,	great-ness	plain,	plain-ness
rash,	rash-ness	sound,	sound-ness
bald,	bald-ness	rough,	rough-ness
hoarse,	hoarse-ness	self-ish,	self-ish-ness
blood-y,	blood-i-ness	come-ly.	come-li-ness

mis-er-a-ble,	mis-er-a-ble-ness
for-mi-da-ble,	for-mi-da-ble-ness
gra-cious,	gra-cious-ness
fa-vor-a-ble,	fa-vor-a-ble-ness
of-fen-sive,	of-fen-sive-ness

An Easy Standard of Pronunciation.

Example VII.

Words formed by *ish*, denoting quality, or a small degree of it.

ape,	a-pish	white,	whi-tish
wasp,	wasp-ish	blue,	blu-ish
wag,	wag-gish	black,	black-ish
block,	block-ish	pur-ple,	pur-plish
sour,	sour-ish	gray,	gray-ish
sweet,	sweet-ish	clown,	clown-ish

Example VIII.

Words formed by *less*, denoting destitution or absence.

art,	art-less	num-ber,	num-ber-less
grace,	grace-less	mo-tion,	mo-tion-less
shape,	shape-less	mea-sure,	mea-sure-less
need,	need-less	fa-ther,	fa-ther-less
heed,	heed-less	moth-er,	moth-er-less
care,	care-less	pray-er,	pray-er-less

Example IX.

Words formed by *al*, denoting quality, and by *some*, denoting fulness.

frac-tion,	frac-tion-al	glad,	glad-some
doc-trine,	doc-trin-al	loath,	loath-some
crime,	crim-in-al	frol-ick,	frol-ick-some
na-tion,	na-tion-al	de-light,	de-light-some

Example X.

Words formed by *ous*, and *ive*, denoting quality.

grace,	gra-cious	sport,	sport-ive
glo-ry,	glo-ri-ous	ex-pense,	ex-pens-ive
hu-mor,	hu-mor-ous	con-clude,	con-clu-sive
mel-o-dy,	me-lo-di-ous	ex-cess,	ex-cess-ive
har-mo-ny,	har-mo-ni-ous	e-lect,	e-lect-ive
vic-tor,	vic-to-ri-ous	de-cide,	de-ci-sive

An Easy Standard of Pronunciation

EXAMPLE XI.

Words formed by *age*, *ment*, *ence*, and *ance*, denoting state, condition, or action performed, &c.

pa-rent,	par-ent-age	per-form,	per-form-ance
pat-ron,	pat-ron-age	ful-fil,	ful-fil-ment
per-son,	per-son-age	at-tain,	at-tain-ment
car-ry,	car-riage	de-pend,	de-pend-ence
mar-ry,	mar-riage	oc-cur,	oc-cur-rence
re-mit,	re-mit-tance	re-pent,	re-pent-ance

ac-com-plish,   ac-com-plish-ment
com-mand,   com-mand-ment

EXAMPLE XII.

Words ending in *or* or *er*, and *ee*, the former denoting the agent; and the latter the person, to whom an act is done.

les-sor',	les-see'	ap-pel-lor',	ap-pel-lee
do'-nor,	do-nee'	cog-ni-zor',	cog-ni-zee
bail-or',	bail-ee'	in-dors'-er,	in-dors-ee
as-sign-or',	as-sign-ee'	ob-li-gor',	ob-li-gee'
pay'-or,	pay-ee'	mort'-ga-ger,	mort-ga-gee'

EXAMPLE XIII.

Words ending in *ity*, denoting power, capacity, state, &c.

in-firm,	in-firm-i-ty	le-gal,	le-gal-i-ty.
a-ble,	a-bil-i-ty	mor-tal,	mor-tal-i-ty

pos-si-ble,   pos-si-bil-i-ty
con-form,   con-form-i-ty
chris-tian,   chris-tian-i-ty
pop-u-lar,   pop-u-lar-i-ty
sin-gu-lar,   sin-gu-lar-i-ty
fea-si-ble,   fea-si-bil-i-ty
com-pat-i-ble,   com-pat-i-bil-i-ty
im-pen-e-tra-ble, im-pen-e-tra-bil-i-ty

An Easy Standard of Pronunciation.

Example XIV.

Verbs or affirmations, formed by the terminations *ize* and *en*.

Gen-er-al,	gen-er-al-ize	mor-al,	mor-al-ize
le-gal,	le-gal-ize	jour-nal,	jour-nal-ize
tyr-an-ny,	tyr-ran-nize	can-on,	can-on-ize
meth-od,	meth-od-ize	har-mo-ny,	har-mo-nize
au-thor,	an-thor-ize	strait,	strait-en
bas-tard,	bas-tard-ize	wide,	wi-den, or
sys-tem,	sys-tem-ize		wid-en
civ-il,	civ-il-ize	length,	length-en

Example XV.

Words in which the sense is changed by prefixing a syllable, or syllables.

Ap-pear,	dis-ap-pear	grow,	o-ver-grow
al-low,	dis-al-low	look,	o-ver-look
o-bey,	dis-o-bey	run,	o-ver-run
o-blige,	dis-o-blige	take,	o-ver-take
es-teem,	dis-es-teem	throw,	o-ver-throw
pos-sess,	dis-pos-sess	turn,	o-ver-turn
ap-ply,	mis-ap-ply	ad-mit,	re-ad-mit
be-have,	mis-be-have	as-sume,	re-as-sume
in-form,	mis-in-form	em-bark,	re-em-bark
de-ceive,	un-de-ceive	en-force,	re-en-force
work,	un-der-work	add,	su-per-add
op-e-rate,	co-op-e-rate	a-bound,	su-per-a-bound
en-gage,	pre-en-gage	weave,	in-ter-weave
ma-ture,	pre-ma-ture	see,	fore-see
num-ber,	out-num-ber	sight,	fore-sight
run,	out-run	plant,	trans-plant
fee-ble,	en-fee-ble	com-pose,	de-com-pose
no-ble,	en-no-ble	act,	coun-ter-act

An Easy Standard of Pronunciation.

EXAMPLE XVI.

Names formed from qualities by change of termination.

| Long, length | deep, depth | dry, drouth |
| strong, strength | high, heighth | wide, width |

Examples of various derivatives from one root, or radical word.

Boun-ty, boun-te-ous, boun-te-ous-ly, boun-te-ous-ness, boun-ti-ful, boun-ti-ful-ly, boun-ti-ful-ness.

Beau-ty, beau-te-ous, beau-te-ous-ly, beau-te-ous-ness, beau-ti-ful, beau-ti-ful-ly, beau-ti-ful-ness, beau-ti-fy.

Art, art-ful, art-ful-ly, art-ful-ness, art-less, art-less-ly, art-less-ness.

Con-form, con-form-i-ty, con-form-a-ble, con-form-a-bly, con-form-ist, con-form-a-tion, con-form-a-ble-ness.

Press, press-ure, im-press, im-press-ion, im-press-ive, im-press-ive-ly, com-press, com-press-ure, com-press-ion, com-press-i-ble, com-press-i-bil-i-ty, in-com-press-i-ble, in-com-press-i-bil-i-ty, de-press, de-press-ion, sup-press, sup-press-ion.

Grief, griev-ous, griev-ous-ly, griev-ance, ag-grieve.

At-tend, at-tend-ant, at-tend-ance, at-ten-tion, at-ten-tive, at-ten-tive-ly, at-ten-tive-ness.

Fa-vor, fa-vor-ite, fa-vor-a-ble, fa-vor-a-bly, fa-vor-a-ble-ness, fa-vor-it-ism, un-fa-vor-a-ble, un-fa-vor-a-bly, un-fa-vor-a-ble-ness, dis-fa-vor.

An Easy Standard of Pronunciation.

Compound Words.

Ale house	cop per plate	gin ger bread
ap ple tree	day light	grand child
bed fel low	din ing room	New ha ven
bed cham ber	Charles town	New york
bee hive	George town	ink stand
book sell er	dress ing room	ju ry man
but ter milk	drip ping pan	land tax
can dle stick	earth quake	lap dog
chain shot	el bow chair	moon shine
cher ry tree	fer ry man	pa per mill
ches nut tree	fire arms	ti tle page
cop y book	fire shov el	Yale col lege

OBSERVATIONS.

He seldom lives frugally, who lives by chance.

Most men are more willing to indulge in easy vices, than to practice laborious virtues.

A man may mistake the love of virtue for the practice of it ; and be less a good man, than the friend of goodness.

Without frugality, none can be rich ; and with it few would be poor.

Moderation and mildness often effect what cannot be done by force. A Persian writer finely observes, that " a gentle hand leads the elephant himself by a hair."

The most necessary part of learning is to unlearn our errors.

Small parties make up in diligence what they want in numbers.

Some talk of subjects which they do not understand, others praise virtue, who do not practice it

No persons are more apt to ridicule or censure others, than those who are most apt to be guilty of follies and faults.

An Easy Standard of Pronunciation.

TABLE XLVII.

Irregular words, not comprised in the foregoing tables.

Written.	Pronounced.	Written.	Pronounced.
A ny	en ny	isle	ile
bat teau	bat to	isl and	ile and
beau	bo	ma ny	men ny
beaux	boze	o cean	o shun
been	bin	says	sez
bu reau	bu ro	said	sed
bu ry	ber ry	sous	soo
bu sy	biz zy	su gar	shoog ar
co lo nel	cur nel	vis count	vi count
haut boy	ho boy	wo men	wim in

Written.	Pronounced.
Ap ro pos	ap pro po
bel les let tres	bel let ter
bu si ness	biz ness
flam beau	flam bo
che vaux de frise	shev o de freeze
en ten dre	en taun der
port man teau	port man ter
right eous	ri chus

The compounds and derivatives follow the same rule.

OBSERVATIONS.

Seek a virtuous man for your friend, for a vicious man can neither love long nor be long beloved.—The friendships of the wicked are conspiracies against morality and social happiness.

Mòre persons seek to live long, though long life is not in their power; than to live well, though a good life depends on their own will.

An Easy Standard of Pronunciation.

USEFUL LESSONS.

JOHN can tell how many square rods of ground make an acre. Let me hear him. Three feet make a yard ; five yards and a half make a rod or perch ; forty square rods make a rood or one quarter of an acre, and one hundred and sixty square rods make an acre. One team will plow an acre in a day—sometimes more.

In solids, forty feet of round timber, or fifty feet of hewn timber, make a ton. A cord of wood contains one hundred and twenty-eight solid feet ; that is, a pile four feet high, four feet wide, and eight feet long.

In cloth measure, two inches and a fourth make a nail —four nails, one quarter of a yard—thirty-six inches, or three feet, make a yard—three quarters of a yard make an ell Flemish—and five quarters make an English ell.

Let us examine the weights used in our own country. How are heavy goods weighed ? By avoirdupois weight—in which sixteen drams make an ounce—sixteen ounces, one pound—twenty-eight pounds, one quarter of a hundred—four quarters, or one hundred and twelve pounds, make a hundred—and twenty hundreds, one ton. By this weight, are sold, hay, sugar, coffee, and all heavy goods and metals, except gold and silver.

What is troy weight? It is that by which is estimated the quantity of gold and silver, jewelry, and the drugs sold by the druggist and apothecary. In troy weight, twenty-four grains make a pennyweight—twenty pennyweights, one ounce—and twelve ounces, one pound. These are the divisions used by the silversmith and jeweller. But the apothecary uses a different division, and in his weight, twenty grains make a scruple—three scruples, one dram—eight drams, one ounce—and, twelve ounces, one pound.

The dollar is one hundred cents; but the value of a pound, shilling, and penny, is different in different states, and in England. English money is called Sterling—one dollar is four shillings and six pence sterling—in New-England and Virginia, it is six shillings—in New-York and North Carolina, it is eight shillings—in New Jersey, Pennsylvania, Delaware and Maryland, it is seven shi''' gs and six pence—in South Carolina and Georgia, it is four ɔs and eight pence. But these differences give great tr l will soon be laid aside as useless ;—all money wŏ, ' ɔ dollars and cents.

An Easy Standard of Pronunciation.

INHABITANTS OF THE UNITED STATES.

Census in	1790	1800	1810	1820
Vermont	85,539	154,465	217,895	235,764
New-Hampshire . . .	141,885	183,858	214,460	244,161
Maine	96,540	151,719	228,705	298,335
Massachusetts	378,787	422,845	472,040	523,287
Rhode Island	68,825	69,122	76,931	83,059
Connecticut	237,946	251,002	261,942	275,248
New-York	340,120	586,050	959,049	1,372,812
New-Jersey	184,139	211,149	245,562	277,575
Pennsylvania	434,373	602,545	810,091	1,049,398
Delaware	59,094	64,273	72,674	72,749
Maryland	319,728	353,968	380,546	407,350
Virginia	747,610	886,149	974,622	1,065,366
North-Carolina	393,951	478,103	555,500	638,829
South-Carolina	249,073	345,591	415,115	490,309
Georgia	82,548	162,686	252,433	346,989
Kentucky	73,677	220,959	406,511	564,317
Territory N. W. of Ohio	35,691	45,365		
	3,929,326			
Of these are slaves 697,696				
Indiana		5,641	24,520	147,178
Mississippi		8,850	40,352	75,448
Tennessee		105,602	261,727	422,813
		5,309,758		
Of these are slaves 894,452				
Ohio			230,760	581,434
Louis. and Orleans Ter.			97,401	153,407
Illinois			12,282	55,211
Michigan Territory .			4,762	8,896
District of Columbia .			24,023	33,039
Of these are slaves 1,191,364			7,239,903	
Alabama				127,901
Missouri				66,586
Grand Total .				734

An Easy Standard of Pronunciation.

TABLE XLVIII.

The most usual Names of Men, accented.

Aa' ron	Dan' iel	Hugh
A' bel	Da' vid	Ho ra' tio
A' bram	Den' nis	Hor' ace
A' bra ham		Hez e ki' ah
Ad' am	Ed' mund	
Al' bert	Ed' ward	I' saac
Al' len	Ed' win	Is' rael
Al ex an' der	Ed' gar	Ich' a bod
Al' fred	Eg' bert	
Am' brose	E le a' zar	Ja' bez
A' mos	El' dad	Ja' cob
An' drew	E' li	James
An' tho ny	E li' as	Jef frey
Ar' chi bald	E li' zur	Job
Ar' nold	E li' sha	Jo' el
Ar' thur	E liph' a let	John
Au' stin	E' noch	Jo' nas
A' sa hel	E' phraim	Jo' seph
A' saph	E ze' ki el	Jo si' ah
A' sa	E ras' tus	Josh' u a
Ash' er	Ez' ra	Jude
	Eb e ne' zer	Jus' tus
		Jer e mi' ah
Bar' na bas	Fran' cis	Jon' a than
Ben' ja min	Fred' er ic	Ja' red
Ben' net		Jes' se
Ber' nard	Ga' briel	
Brad' ford	George	Leon' ard
	Gid' e on	Lew' is
Ca' leb	Gil' bert	Lu' cius
Charles	Giles	Luke
Chris' to pher	God' frey	Lem' u el
Cor ne' li us	Greg' o ry	Le' vi
Clark		Lu' ther
Cyp' ri an	Hen' ry	

An Easy Standard of Pronunciation.

Mark	Pe' ter	Ste' phen
Mar' tin	Paul	Si' las
Mat' thew	Phil' ip	
Mi' chael	Phin' e as	The' o dore
Miles		The oph' i lus
Mor' gan	Ralph	Thom' as
Mo' ses	Reu' ben	Tim' o thy
Me' dad	Rich' ard	Ti' tus
	Rob' ert	
	Ro" ger	U ri' ah
Na' than	Ru' fus	
Na than' iel		Val' en tine
Ne he mi' ah		Vin' cent
Nich' o las	Sam' u el	
Nor' man	Seth	Wal' ter
	Sil ves' ter	Will' iam
	Sim' e on	
Ob a di' ah	Si' mon	Za' dok
Ol' i ver	Sol' o mon	Zech a ri' ah

Names of Women.

Ab' i gail	Dor' cas	Grace
A' my	Dor' o thy	
Ann	De' li a	Han' nah
An' na		Har' ri et
An' nis	El' ea nor	Hel' en
A me' lia	E li' za	Hen ri et' ta
	E liz' a beth	Hes' ter
Bridg' et	Em' ma	Hul' dah
Be lin' da	Em' i ly	
	Es' ther	Is' a bel
Car' o line	Eu' nice	
Cla ris' sa	E mil' ia	Jane
Ce' li a		Je mi' ma
	Faith	Jen' net
Deb' o rah	Flo' ra	Ju' li a
Di' nah	Fran' ces	Ju li an' a

An Easy Standard of Pronunciation.

Kath' a rine	Ma ri' a	Re bec' ca
		Ruth
Love	Nan' cy	Rose
Lu' cy		
Lyd' ia	Pa' tience	Sa' rah
Lu cre' tia	Pe nel' o pe	So phi' a
Lu cin' da	Phe' be	Sal' ly
	Phil' lis	Su san' nah
Ma' bel	Pris cil' la	Su' san
Mar' ga ret	Pru' dence	
Mar' tha		Tem' per ance
Ma' ry	Ra' chel	Ur su' la

Derivatives from Names.

Am' mon,	Am' mon ite
Ca' naan,	Ca' naan ite
E' phraim,	E' phraim ite
Mo' ab,	Mo' ab ite
Cal' vin,	Cal' vin ist
Lu' ther,	Lu' ther an
Is' rael,	Is' rael ite
Rome,	Ro' man
Cor' inth,	Co rinth' i an
Ath' ens,	A the' ni an
Ha' gar,	Ha' gar enes
Ga la' tia,	Ga la' tians
Sa ma' ri a,	Sa mar' i tans
Am' a lek,	Am' a lek ite
E' dom,	E' dom ite
Beth' le hem,	Beth' le hem ite
Lon' don,	Lon' don er
Par' is,	Pa ris' ian
Ben' ja min,	Ben' ja min ite
Reu' ben,	Reu' ben ite
Jew,	Jew' ish
New ton,	New to n an

An Easy Standard of Pronunciation

A lex an' dri a,	A lex an' dri an
Ci'' ce ro,	Ci'' ce ro' ni an
Co per' nic us,	Co per' nic an
Ep i cu' rus,	Ep i cu' re an
Gal' i lee,	Gal i le' an
Ma hom' et,	Ma hom' e tan
Sad' du cee,	Sad du ce' an
Phar' i see,	Phar i sa' ic
Pla' to,	Pla ton'-ic
Pla' to nism,	Pla' ton ist
Chal de' a,	Chal de' an
Cy re' ne,	Cy re' ni an
Gil' e ad,	Gil' e ad ite
Her' od,	He ro' di ans
Ish' ma el,	Ish' ma el ite
Mid' i an,	Mid' i an ite
Tyre,	Tyr' i an

TABLE XLIX.

*Names of the principal Countries on the Eastern Conti-
nent, the adjective belonging to each, the name of the
People, and the chief Town or City—accented.*

Country.	Adjective.	People.	Chief Cities.
A' sia,	A siat' ic,	A siat' ics,	
Af' ri ca,	Af' ri can,	Af' ri cans,	
Aus' tri a,	Aus' tri an,	Aus' tri ans,	Vi en' na
A ra' bi a,	Ar' a bic, / A ra' bi an,	A ra' bi ans, / or A' rabs,	Mec' ca
Al gie'rs,	Al ge ri'ne,	Al ge ri'nes,	Al gi'ers
Brit' ain,	Brit' ish,	Brit' ons,	Lon' don
Eng' land,	Eng' lish,	Eng' lish,	
Scot' land,	Scotch,	Scots,	Ed' in burgh
I re land,	rish,	rish. or / I' rish men,	Dub' lin
Hi ber' ni a,	Hi ber' ni an,	Hi ber' nians,	

An Easy Standard of Pronunciation.

Country	Adjective.	People.	Chief Cities.
Wales,	Welch,	Welch' men,	
Bo he' mia,	Bo he' mi an,	Bo he' mi ans,	Prague
Chi' na,	{ Chi ne'se, Chi' na,	Chi ne'se,	Pe' kin
Cor' si ca	Cor si can,	Cor' si cans,	Bas' tia
Den mark,	Da' nish,	Danes,	Co pen ha' gen
E gypt,	E gyp' tian,	E gyp' tians,	{ Ca'i ro, or Ca'i ra
Eu rope,	Eu ro pe' an,	Eu ro pe' ans,	
Flan' ders,	Flem' ish,	Flem' ings,	} Brus' sels
Bel' gi um,	Bel' gi an,	Bel' gi ans,	
France,	French,	French,	} Par' is
Gaul,	{ Gal' lic, or Gal' li can,	Gauls,	
Fran co' ni a,	Fran co' ni an,	Fran co' ni ans,	Wurts' burg
Ger' ma ny,	{ Ger' man, Ger man'ic,	Ger' mans,	Vi en' na
Ba va' ri a,	Ba va' ri an,	Ba va' ri ans,	Mu' nich
Gen' o a,	Gen o e'se,	Gen o e'se,	} Gen' o a
Li gu' ri a,	Li gu' ri an,	Li gu' ri ans,	
Greece,	Gre' cian,	Greeks,	Ath' ens
Hol' land,	Dutch,	Dutch, or Hol' land ers,	} Am'ster dam
Ba ta' vi a,	Ba ta' vi an,	Ba ta' vi ans,	Hague
Hun' ga ry,	Hun ga' ri an,	Hun ga' ri ans,	{ Pres' burg, or Bu' da
It' a ly,	{ I tal' ian, I tal' ic,	} I tal' ian,	Rome
I'ce land,	Ice land ic,	I'ce land ers,	
In' di a,	{ In' di an, Hin' du, Hin' doo,	In' di an, Hin' dus, Hin' doos,	} Del' hi Cal cut' ta
In du' stan,	Gen' too,	Gen' toos,	Ma drass'
Ja pan',	Jap an e'se,	Jap an e'se,	
Mi lan',	Mi lan e'se,	Mi lan e'se,	Mi lan'
Mo roc' co,	Moor' ish,	Moors,	Fez
Na' ples,	Ne a pol' i tan,	Ne a pol' i tans,	Na' ples

An Easy Standard of Pronunciation.

Country.	Adjective.	People.	Chief Cities.
Nor' way,	Nor we' gi an,	Nor we' gi ans,	Ber' gen
Per' sia,	Per' sian,	Per' sians,	Is pa han'
Pied mont',	Pied mon te'se	Pied mon te'se	Tu rin'
Po' land,	Po' lish,	{ Po' land ers, or Poles,	War' saw
Por' tu gal,	Por tu gues e,	Por' tu guese,	Lis' bon
Prus' sia,	Prus' sian,	Prus' sians,	Ber' lin
Rus' sia,	Rus' sian,	Rus' sians,	Pe' ters burg
Si'' ci ly,	Si cil' i an,	Si cil' i ans,	Pa ler' mo
Spain,	Span' ish,	Span' iards,	Ma drid'
Sar din' i a,	Sar din' i an,	Sar din' i ans,	Cag li a' ri
Swe' den,	Swe' dish,	Swedes,	Stock' holm
Swit' zer land,	Swiss,	Swiss,	{ Bern, or Bas' il
Sax' o ny,	Sax' on,	Sax' ons,	Dres' den
Swa' bi a,	Swa' bi an,	Swa' bi ans,	Augs' burg
Tur' key,	Turk' ish,	Turks,	{ Con' stan ti- no' ple
Tar' ta ry,	{ Tar' tar, Tar ta' ri an,	Tar' tars,	{ To bol' ski Thi' bet
Tu' nis,	Tu nis' ian,	Tu nis' ians,	Tu' nis
Tus' ca ny,	Tus' can,	Tus' cans,	Flor' ence
Si am',	Si am e'se,	Si am e'se,	Si am'
Ton' quin,	Ton quin e'se,	Ton quin e'se,	Tong too'
Ven' ice,	Ve ne' tian,	Ve ne' tians,	Ven' ice

In America

A mer' i ca,	A mer' i can,	A mer' i cans
States.	**Chief Towns.**	**People.**
New Hamp' shire,	Po'rts mouth	
Maine,	Po'rt land	
Mas sa chu' setts,	Bos' ton,	Bos to' ni ans
Ver mont',	{ Ben' ning ton, Mont pe' lier, Wind' sor,	} Ver mont' ers

An Easy Standard of Pronunciation.

States	Chief Towns.	People.
Rhode i's land,	Prov' i dence & New' port,	Rhode i's land ers
Con nec' ti cut,	Hart' ford, New Ha' ven and New Lon' don	
New York,	New York and Al' ba ny,	New York' ers
New Jer' sey,	Tren' ton, E liz' a beth town, Prince' ton, and New' ark	
Penn syl va' ni a,	Phil a del' phi a, Lan' cas ter,	Penn syl va'- ni ans
Del' a ware,	Wil' ming ton and Do' ver	
Ma' ry land,	Bal' ti more and An nap' o lis,	Ma' ry land ers
Vir gin' i a,	Rich' mond, Al ex an' dri a, Nor' folk,	Vir gin' i ans
North Car o li' na,	New' bern, Wil' ming ton, E' den ton,	Car o lin' i ans
South Car o li' na,	Charles' ton, Co lum' bi a,	
Ge or' gi a,	Sa van' na, Au gus' ta,	Ge or gi ans
Ken tuck' y,	Lex' ing ton,	Ken tuck' i ans
Ten nes see',	Nash' ville,	Ten nes se' ans
O hi' o,	Co lum' bus	
Lou is ian' a,	New Or' leans,	Lou is ia' ni ans

British, Spanish, and Portuguese America

Provinces.	Chief Towns.	People
Can' a da,	Que bec',	Ca na' di ans
New Bruns' wick,	St. Johns,	
No' va Sco' tia,	Hal' i fax,	
E. Flor' i da,	Au gus ti'ne,	
W. Flor' i da,	Pen sa co' la,	

An Easy Standard of Pronunciation.

Provinces.	Chief towns	People.
Mex' i co,	Mex' i co,	Mex' i cans
Chi' li,	St. Ja' go,	Chil' i ans
Pe ru',	Li' ma,	Pe ru' vi ans
Qui' to,	Qui' to,	
Par a gua'y,	Buen' os Ayres,	
Bra zil',	St. Sal va do're,	Bra zil' i ans

————

TABLE L.

Chief Rivers on the Eastern Continent.

IN EUROPE.

Dan' ube	Loire	Scheldt*
Don, or	Med' way	Sev' ern
Ta na' is	Maes	Shan' non
Drave	Mo sell'e	Seine
Du' ro	Nie' per, or	Soane
Dwi' na	Bo rist' he nes	Tay
E' bro	Nie' men	Ta' gus
Elbe	Nie' ster	Thames
Eu ro' tis	O' der	Ti' ber
Ga ro'nne	Pe ne' us	Vis' tu la
Gua' del quiv ier	Po	Vol' ga
Gua di an' a	Rhone	We' ser
Hum' ber	Rhine	

* Pronounced Shelt.

————

IN ASIA

A rax' es	Ir' tis	O 'by
A' va	Jen i see'	Ox' us
Cu ban'	Kur, or	Pe gu'
Eu phra' tes	Cy' rus	Rha
Gan' ges	Me an' der	Ti' gris
Ma' lys	Me non'	Yel' low, or
In' dus, or Sind	Me con'	Ho ang' ho

An Easy Standard of Pronunciation.

IN AFRICA.

Ba gra' da, *or*	Sen e gal'	Or' ange
Me ger' da	Ni' ger, *or*	Gau lit'z
Nile	Jc. i ba'	

Oceans.

At lan' fic	Pa cif' ic	In' di an

Seas.

Bal' tic	Eu'x ine	Me o' tis, *or*
Cas' pi an	Med i ter ra' ne an	A' zoph

Bays and Gulfs.

A dri at' ic	Cal i for' ni a	Fun' dy
Baf' fin's	Ches' a peak	Hud' son's
Bis' cay	Cha leu'r	Mex' i co
Both' ni a	Fin' land	Ri ga'

Lakes in Europe and Asia.

As phal' tis	Ge ne' va	Lu ga' na
Bai' kal	Gar' da	Mag gi o're
Co' mo	Is' co	O ne' ga
Con' stance	La do' ga	Wi nan'

Mountains in Europe, Africa, and Asia

Alps	Car' mel	Ju' ra
Ap' pe nines	Et' na	Py re nee's
Ar' ra rat	Hec' la	Si' nai
At' las	Ho' reb	Tau' rus
Ce ven' nes	I' da	Ve su' vi us
Cau' ca sus		

In America.

An' des, *or*	Al le ga' ny	Kit ta kin' ny
Cor dil' ler as	Kaats' kill	O le roy'

An Easy Standard of Pronunciation.

Chief Rivers in America.

Am' a zon, *or*
Mar' a non
Al' ba ny
Ap a lach' y
Ap' a lach' i co' la
Ar' kan saw
Al ta ma haw'
An dros cog' gin

Buf' fa lo

Cum' ber land
Chat ta ho' chy
Clar' en don, *or*
Cape Fear
Chow an'
Con nec' ti cut
Co lum' bi a, *or*
Ta coo' chy
Chau di e're

Del' a ware

E dis' to
Elk

Flint

Hack' en sac
Hou sa ton' uc
Hock hock' ing
Hud' son

Il le nois'
I' ro quois, *or*
St. Law' rence

Ja ne'i ro
James, *or*
Pow hat tan'

Kan ha' way
Ken tuc' ky,
Ken ne bec'

Lick' ing
La moil'

Mis si sip' pi
Mis so rie'
Musk ing' um
Mi am' i
Mo bill'
Mis sisk' o
Mer' ri mac
Moose
Ma ken' zie

Nuse
Nel' son

O ro no'ke
O hi' o
O gee' chy
On' ion

Par a gua'y, *or*
Plate
Po to' mac
Pearl
Pas cat' a way
Pe nob' scot
Pas sa' ic

Ph dee'

Roan o'ke
Rap pa han' noc
Sar' i ton

Sa van' na
San tee'
Sa lu' da
Sa til' la
Sus que han' na
Schu'yl kill
Sci o' ta
Sau' co
Scoo' duc
St. John
St. Mary
Sev' ern
Sas ka shaw' in
So rell'
Sag u nau'

Ten nes see'
Tu' gu lo
Tom big' by

Un' ji ga
U ta was'

Wat ter ee'
Wau' bosh

York
Ya zoo'

An Easy Standard of Pronunciation.

Lakes in America.

Cay u' ga	Moose' head	Su pe' ri or
Can an dai' gua	Mem fre ma' gog	Tez cu' co
Cham pla'in	Ot se' go	Um' ba gog
E' rie	O nei' da	Win' ni pis i o' gy
George	On ta' ri o	Win' ni pic
Hu' ron	On an da' go	Wa' que fa no' ga
Mich i gan'	Sen' e ka	or O' ka fa no' ke

TABLE LI.

Names of Cities, Towns, Counties, Rivers, Mountains, Lakes, Islands, Bays, &c. in America.

The following have the accent on the first syllable.

A	An do ver	Av on
Ab' er corn	An ge lo	Ayers ton
Ab ing don	An ge los	
Ab ing ton	An trim	**B**
Ab se con	An vill	Bairds town
Ac ton	Aq ue fort	Ba kers field
Ad ams	Arm strong	Ba kers town
Ac worth	Ar ling ton	Ball town
Al ba ny	Ar row sike	Bal ti more
Al bi on	Ar u ba	Ban gor
Al ford	Ash burn ham	Bar ba ra
Al lens town	Ash by	Bar nard
All burg	Ash field	Bar na velt
Al lo way	Ash ford	Bar ne gat
All saints	Ash ton	Bar net
Alms bu	Ash we lot	Barn sta ble
Al stead	As sa bet	Barn sted
Am boy	A thol	Bar re
Am e lins	At kin son	Bar rets ton
Ame well	At tle bo rough	Bar ring ton
Am herst	Av a lon	Bart let
Am ster dam	A ve ril	Bar ton

An Easy Standard of Pronunciation.

Bart	Bloom field	Bridge port
Bath	Bloom ing dale	Brid port
Bat ten kill	Blount	Brim field
Bea ver	Blounts ville	Bris tol
Beau fort	Blue hill	Brom ley
Beck et	Bol in broke	Brook field
Bed ford	Bol ton	Brook lyn
Bed min ster	Bom bay	Broth er ton
Beek man	Bom ba zin	Brough ton
Belch er	Bon a ven ture	Brown field
Bel fast	Bon a vis ta	Brun ners town
Bel grade	Bon ham town	Browns ville
Bel ling ham	Boone ton	Bruns wick
Ben ning ton	Boons bo *rough*	Bru tus
Ben e dict	Bop quam	Buck land
Ben son	Bor den town	Buc kles town
Ber gen	Bot e tourt	Bucks town
Berk ley	Bot tle hill	Buck town
Berk shire	Bound brook	Bull skin
Ber lin	Bour bon	Burke
Ber nards town	Bow doin	Bur ling ton
Bern	Bow doin ham	Bur ton
Ber wic	Bow ling green	Bush town
Beth a ny	Box bo *rough*	Bush wick
Beth el	Box ford	Bus tard
Beth le hem	Boyl ston	But ier
Bev er ly	Boz rah	But ter field
Bil lings port	Brad ford	But ter hill
Bir ming ham	Brain tree	Bux ton
Black stone	Bran don	Buz zards bay
Bla den	Bran dy wine	By ber ry
Bla dens burg	Bran ford	Bye field
Blan ca	Brat tle bo *rough*	By ram
Blan co	Breck nock	
Bland ford	Brent wood	C
Bled soe	Bre ton	Cab ot
Blen heim	Bridge town	Ca diz
Block ley	Bridge wa ter	Cal ais

An Easy Standard of Pronunciation.

Cal ders burg
Cal la o
Cal vert
Cam bridge
Cam den
Camp bell
Cam po bel lo
Camp ton
Ca naan
Can dia
Can ons burg
Can so
Can ter bu ry
Can ton
Car di gan
Car ibs
Car los
Car mel
Car mel o
Car ne ro
Carns ville
Car o lin
Car ter
Car ter et
Car ters ville
Car ver
Cas co
Cas tle ton
Cas tle town
Cas well
Ca to
Cav en dish
Cay mans
Ce cil
Cen ter
Cham bers burg
Chap el hill
Chance ford

Charles ton
Charles town
Charle ton
Char lotte
Char lottes ville
Chat ham
Chelms ford
Chel sea
Chel ten ham
Chesh ire
Ches ter
Ches ter field
Ches ter town
Chick o py
Chi ches ter
Chip pe ways
Chil mark
Chit ten den
Choc taws
Chris tians burg
Chris tian sted
Chris to phers
Church town
Ci'' ce ro
Clar en don
Clarks burg
Clarkes town
Clarkes ville
Clav er ack
Clin ton
Clinch
Clos ter
Cob ham
Co bles hill
Cock burne
Cock er mouth
Cooy mans
Cokes bu ry

Col ches ter
Cole brook
Con cord
Con way
Coots town
Cor inth
Cor nish·
Corn wall
Cort landt
Cov en try
Cow pens
Cox hall
Crab or chard
Cran ber ry
Cra ney
Crans ton
Cra ven
Craw ford
Cross wicks
Cro ton
Crown point
Croy den
Cul pep per
Cum ber land
Cum ming ton
Cus co
Cush e tunk
Cush ing
Cus sens
Cus si tah

D

Dal ton
Dan bu ry
Dan by
Dan vers
Dan ville
Dar by

An Easy Standard of Pronunciation.

Da ri en
Dar ling ton
Dart mouth
Dau phin
Da vid son
Ded ham
Deer field
Deer ing
Den nis
Den ton
Dept ford
Der by
Der ry
Der ry field
Dig by
Digh ton
Dis mal
Don ne gal
Dor ches ter
Dor lach
Dor set
Doug las
Down ings
Dra cut
Dres den
Dro more
Drum mond
Dry den
Duck creek
Duck trap
Dud ley
Dum mer
Dum mers town
Dun cans burg
Dun der burg
Dun sta ble
Dur ham
Duch ess

Dux bo rough
Dux bu ry
Dy ber ry

E

Eas ter ton
East ham
East on
East town
Ea ton
Ea ton town
E den
Edes ton
Ed gar ton
Edge comb
Edge field
Edge mont
Ef fing ham
Egg har bor
Eg mont
Eg re mont
El bert
El bert son
Elk
Elk horn
Elk ridge
Elk ton
El ling ton
El lis
El more
Em mits burg
En field
En glish town
E no
E nos burg
Ep ping
Ep som
Er rol

Er vin
Es qui maux
Es sex
Est her town
Eus tace
E vans ham
Eves ham
Ex e ter

F

Fa bi us
Fair fax
Fair field
Fair lee
Falk land
Fal mouth
Fals ing ton
Fan net
Fa quier
Far ming ton
Fay ette ville
Fays town
Fed er als burg
Fells point
Fer ris burg
Fin cas tle
Find ley
Fish ers field
Fish kill
Fitch burg
Flat land
Flem ing ton
Fletch er
Flints ton
Flow er ton
Floyd
Flush ing
Fol low field

An Easy Standard of Pronunciation.

For est er ton
Fram ing ham
Fran ces town
Fran cis burg
Fran cois
Frank fort
Frank lin
Franks town
Fred e ri ca
Fred e rick
Fred e ricks burg
Fred e ricks town
Free hold
Free port
Free town
Fried burg
Fried land
Fried en stadt
Fry burg
Frow sack

G

Gal en
Gal lo way
Gal way
Gard ner
Gas pee
Gates
Gay head
George town
Ger man town
Ger ma ny
Ger ry
Get tys burg
Gill
Gil lo ri
Gil man town
Gil son

Glas gow
Glas ten bu ry
Glouces ter
Glov er
Glynn
Goffs town
Golds burg
Gol phing ton
Gooch land
Gor ham
Go shen
Gos port
Go tham
Graf ton
Grain ger
Gren a dines
Gran ville
Gray
Green burg
Green cas tle
Green field
Green land
Greens burg
Greens ville
Green ville
Green wich
Green wood
Gregs town
Gro ton
Gry son
Guil ford
Gur net
Guys burg

H

Hack ets town
Had dam
Had don field

Had ley
Ha gars town
Hal lam
Hal low el
Ham den
Ham burg
Ham il ton
Ham mels town
Hamp shire
Hamp sted
Hamp ton
Han cock
Han nahs town
Han ni bal
Han o ver
Har din
Hard wick
Har dy
Har dys town
Har ford
Har lem
Har mo ny
Har mar
Har pers field
Har ple
Harps well
Har ring ton
Har ris burg
Har ri son
Har rods burg
Hart ford
Hart land
Har vard
Har wich
Har win ton
Hat burg
Hat field
Hat cl y

An Easy Standard of Pronunciation.

Hat te ras	Hol lis ton	**J**
Hav er ford	Hols ton	Jack son
Ha ver hill	Ho mer	Jack sons burg
Hav er straw	Hon ey goe	Jaf frey
Haw	Hooks town	Ja go
Hawke	Hoo sac	James
Haw kins	Hop kin ton	James town
Haw ley	Hop kins	Jay
Hay cock	Hope well	Jef fer son
Heath	Horn town	Jek yl
He bron	Horse neck	Jenk in town
Hec tor	Hors ham	Jer e mic
Hei dle berg	Hor ton	Jer i co
Hurl gate	Ho sac	Jer sey
Hem lock	Hub bard ton	Johns bu ry
Hemp field	Hub ber ton	John son
Hen m ker	Hughs burg	John son burg
Hen ri co	Hum mels town	Johns town
Hen ry	Hun ger ford	Johns ton
Her ke mer	Hun ter don	Jones
Hert ford	Hun ters town	Jones burg
Hi ats town	Hun ting don	Jop pa
Hick mans	Hunt ing ton	Jore
High gate	Hunts burg	Ju dith
High land	Hunts ville	Ju lian
Hills dale	Hur ley	Ju li et
Hills burg	Hydes park	Ju ni us
Hill town		
Hines burg	**I**	**K**
Hing ham	Ib ber ville	Kaats kill
Hins dale	In gra ham	Keene
Hi ram	In ver ness	Kel lys burn
Hit ton	Ips wich	Ken net
Ho bok	I ras burg	Ken no mic
Hol den	Ire dell	Ken sing ton
Hol der ness	Ir vin	Kent
Hol land	Isles burg	Kep lers
Hol lis	I slip	Ker is son gar

An Easy Standard of Pronunciation.

Ker shaw
Kick a muit
Kil ling ly
Kil ling ton
Kil ling worth
Kim bec
King less
Kings bu ry
Kings ton
King wood
Kit te ry
*K*now*l* ton
*K*nox
*K*nou*l* ton
*K*nox vill*e*
Kort right

L

Lab ra dor
Lam pe ter
Lam prey
Lan cas ter
Lang don
Lanes bo rou*gh*
Lan sing burg
Law renc*e*
Lau rens
Lea cock
Lees burg
Leb a non
Leeds
Le hi*gh*
Le*ices* ter
Lem ing ton
Lemps ter
Len ox
Le o gane
Leom in ster

Le on
Leon ards town
Lev er ett
Le vi
Lew is
Lew is burg
Lew is town
Lex ing ton
Ley den
Lib er ty
Lich te nau
Lick ing
Lim er ick
Lime stone
Lin col*n*
Lin col*n* town
Lind ley
Litch field
Lit tle burg
Lit tle ton
Liv er more
Liv er pool
Liv ing ston
Lock*e*
Lock arts burg
Lo gan
Logs town
Lon don der ry
Lon don grove
Look out
Lou don
Loch a bar
Lou is vill*e*
Lou is town
Loy al soc
Lud low
Lum ber ton
Lu nen burg

Lur gan
Lut ter lock
Ly man
Lyme
Lynch burg
Lynde burg
Lyn den
Lyun
Lynn field
Ly ons
Lys tra

M

Mac o keth
Mac o pin
Mad bu ry
Mad i son
Maid stone
Maine
Make field
Mal a bar
Mal den
Mar o nec
Man ca
Man chac
Man ches ter
Man heim
Man li us
Man ning ton
Man or
Man sel
Mans field
Mar ble ton
Mar ga rets vill*e*
Mar got
Marl bo rou*gh*
Mar low
Mar p!e

An Easy Standard of Pronunciation.

Marsh field	Mil lers town	Nau ga tuc
Mar tic	Mil stone	Nave sink
Mar tin	Mil town	Naz a reth
Mar tins burg	Mil ton	Ned dick
Mar tins ville	Min gun	Need ham
Mas co my	Min goes	Nel son
Ma son	Min sink	Nes co pec
Mas sac	Mis tic	Nesh a noc
Mas ti gon	Mo hawk	Nev er sink
Mat thews	Monk ton	New ark
May field	Mon mouth	New burg
Mead ville	Mon son	New bu ry
Meck len burg	Mon ta gue	New bu ry port
Med field	Mont mo rin	New found land
Med ford	Moore	New ing ton
Med way	Moore field	New lin
Mend ham	Moose head	New mar ket
Men don	More land	New ton
Mer cer	More	New town
Mer cers burg	Mor gan	Nit ta ny
Mer e dith	Mor gan town	Nix on ton
Mer i meg	Mor ris town	No ble burg
Me ri on	Mor ris ville	None such
Me ro	Moul ton bery	Noot ka
Mes sers burg	Mul li cus	Nor ridge woc
Mid dle bo rough	Mun cy	Nor ri ton
Mid dle bu ry	Mur frees burg	North bo rough
Mid dle field	My ers town	North bridge
Mid dle hook		North field
Mid dle berg	**N**	North port
Mid dle burg	Nan je my	North wood
Mid dle sex	Nan ti coke	Nor ton
Mid dle ton	Nan ti mill	Nor walk
Mid dle town	Nash	Nor way
Mid way	Nash u a	Nor wich
Miff lin	Nas sau	Not ta way
Mil ford	Natch es	Not ting ham
Mil field	Na tick	Nox an

An Easy Standard of Pronunciation.

O
Oak ham
O bed
O bi on
O cri coc
O gle thorp
O hi ope
Old town
Ons low
Or ange
Or ange burg
Or ange town
Or ford
Or le ans
Or ring ton
Or wel
Os na burg
Os si py
Os ti co
O tis field
Ot ta was
Ot ter creek
Ou li out
Ov id
Ox ford

P
Pack ers field
Pac o let
Pal a tine
Palm er
Pam ti co
Pan ton
Pa ri a
Par is
Pax tang
Par sons field
Par tridge field
Pat ter son

Pau ca tuc
Paw ling
Pauls burg
Paw let
Pax ton
Peach am
Pea cock
Pearl
Peeks kill
Pel ham
Pel i can
Pem i gon
Pem broke
Pen dle ton
Pen guin
Pen ning ton
Penns burg
Penns bu ry
Pep in
Pep per el
Pep per el burg
Pe quot
Per ki o my
Per lic an
Per son
Pe ter bo rough
Pe ters burg
Pe ters ham
Pey tons burg
Phil ip
Phil ips burg
Pick ers ville
Pic o let
Pi geon
Pike land
Pi lot town
Pinck ney

Pinck ney ville
Pis to let
Pitt
Pitts burg
Pitts field
Pitts ford
Pitts town
Plain field
Plais tow
Platts burg
Plum sted
Plym outh
Plymp ton
Po land
Pom fret
Pomp ton
Pomp ey
Pop lin
Por pess
Po ter field
Port land
Ports mouth
Pot ters
Pot ters town
Potts grove
Poult ney
Pow nal
Pow nal burg
Prai ry
Pres cott
Pres ton
Pros pect
Prov ince
Prov ince tow
Pru dence
Pur rys burg
Put ney

An Easy Standard of Pronunciation.

Q

Qua ker town
Quee chy
Queens bury
Queens town
Quib ble town
Quin e baug
Quin cy
Quin e paug

R

Ra by
Rad nor
Ra leigh
Ran dolph
Ran dom
Ra pha el
Raph oc
Raw don
Rah way
Ray mond
Rayn ham
Rays town
Read field
Read ing
Red ding
Read ing town
Reeds burg
Reel foot
Reems town
Reis ters town
Rens se laer
Rens se laer wick
Rhine beck
Rich field
Rich mond
Ridge field
Rid ley
Rindge

Rin gos town
Rob ert son
Rob e son
Roch es ter
Rock bridge
Rock fish
Rock ford
Rock hill
Rocking ham
Ro'' gers ville
Rom ney
Rom o pac
Rom u lus
Rose way
Ros sig nol
Rot ter dam
Rowe
Row ley
Rox burg
Rox bu ry
Roy al ton
Roy als ton
Rum ney
Ru pert
Rus sel
Ru ther ford
Ruths burg
Rye
Rye gate

S

Sa lem
Sack ville
Sad bu ry
Sau ga tuc
Sal ford
Salis bu ry
Sam burg
Samp town

Samp son
San born ton
San co ty
Sand gate
San dis field
San down
Sand wick
San dy hook
San dys ton
Sand ford
San ger field
San ta cruse
Sas sa fras
Sau con
Sau kies
Sav age
Sav brook
Scar bo rough
Scars dale
Sho dack
Shen brun
Scoo duc
Schuy ler
Scip i o
Scit u ate
Scriv en
Scroon
Sea brook
Sears burg
Sedg wick
See konk
Se gum
Sen e ka
Sev ern
Se vi er
Shafts bu ry
Sham mo ny
Sham i kin

An Easy Standard of Pronunciation.

Snap leigh	Sole bu ry	Stod dard
ha ron	So lon	Stokes
harks town	Som ers	Stone ham
harps burg	Som er set	Ston ing ton
haw ny	Som ers worth	Sto no
haw nees	Son go	Stou e nuck
heep scut	South bo rough	Stough ton
hef field	South bu ry	Stow
hel burn	South field	Straf·ford
hel by	South ing ton	Stras burg
hen an do ah	South wark	Strat ford
hep herds field	South wick	Strat ham
hep herds town	Span ish town	Strat ton
her burn	Spar ta	Stums town
hip pands town	Spar tan burg	Stur bridge
hip pens burg	Spen cer	Styx
hir·ley	Spots wood	Steu ben ville
hong um	Spring field	Stis sick
hore ham	Spur wing	Sud bu ry
hrews bu ry	Squam	Suf field
hutes bu ry	Staats burg	Suf folk
id ney	Staf ford	Suf frage
ins bu ry	Stam ford	Sul li van
ing sing	Stand ish	Su mans town
in i ca	Stan ford	Sum ner
an pink	Stan wix	Sun a py
kenes burg	Starks burg	Sun bu ry
kup per nong	States burg	Sun cook
kip ton	Staun ton	Sun der land
ku tock	Ster ling	Sur ry
lib town	Steu ben	Sus sex
smith field	Ste vens	Sut ton
smith town	Ste vens burg	Swains cot
smith ville	Ste ven town	Swans burg
smyr na	Ste phen town	Swan sey
show hill	Still wa ter	Swan ton
snow town	Stock bridge	Swan town
so dus	Stock port	Swedes burg

An Easy Standard of Pronunciation.

Syd ney	Trap town	Wad me law
T	Trent	Wads worth
Tal bot	Tren ton	Wad ham
Tam ma ny	Troy	Waits field
Tam worth	Tru ro	Wa jo mic
Ta ney town	Try on	Wake field
Ten saw	Tuck er ton	Wak a maw
Tar bo rough	Tuf ton burg	Wal den
Tar ry town	Tul ly	Wald burg
Taun ton	Tun bridge	Wales
Teach es	Tur bet	Wal ling ford
Tel i co	Tur key	Wall kill
Tem plé	Turn er	Wall pack
Tem ple ton	Twig twees	Wal pole
Tewks bu ry	Tyngs burg	Wal sing ham
Thames	Tyr ing ham	Walt ham
Thet ford	Tyr rel	Wand o
Thom as	U	Want age
Thom as town	Uls ter	Wards burg
Thomp son	Un der hill	Wards bridge
Thorn bu ry	U ni on	Ware
Thorn ton	U ni ty	Ware ham
Thur man	Up ton	War min ster
Tin i cum	U ti ca	Warn er
Tin mouth	U trecht	War ren
Tis bu ry	Ux bridge	War ren ton
Tiz on	V	War ring ton
Tiv er ton	Vas sal burg	War saw
Tol land	Veal town	War wick
Tomp son town	Ver non	Wash ing ton
Tops field	Ver shire	Wa ter burg
Tops ham	Vic to ry	Wa ter bu ry
Tor but	Vin cent	Wa ter ford
Tor ring ton	Vir gil	Wa ter town
Tot te ry	Vol un town	Wa ter vliet
Tow er hill		Waw a sink
Towns end	W	Wayne
Trap	Wades burg	Waynes burg

An Easy Standard of Pronunciation.

Wears	White marsh	Wins low
Weth ers field	Whit pa:ne	Win ter ham
Weï sen berg	White plains	Win throp
Well fleet	Whites town	Win ton
Wells	Whi ting	Wo burn
Wen deh	Whit ting ham	Wol cott
Wen nam	Wick ford	Wolf burg
Went worth	Wil bra ham	Wo mel dorf
We sel	Wilks bar re	Wood bridge
West bo rough	Wili iams burg	Wood bu ry
Wes ter ly	Will iams port	Wood creek
Wes tern	Will iam son	Wood ford
West field	Will iams town	Wood stock
West ford	Wil lin burg	Woods town
West ham	Wil ling ton	Wool wich
West min ster ·	Wii lis	Worces ter
West more	Wil lis ton	Wor thing ton
West more land	Wills burg	Wrent ham
West on	Wil man ton	Wrights burg
West port	Wil ming ton	Wrights town
West town	Wil mot	Wy an dott
Wey mouth	Wil son ville	Wyn ton
Wey bridge	Win chen don	Wythe
Whar ton	Win ches ter	Y
Whate ly	Wind ham	Yad kin
Wheel ing	Win hall	Yar mouth
Whee lock	Win lock	Yonk ers
Whip pa ny	Win ni pec	York
White field	Winns burg	York town

The following have the accent on the second syllable.

A	Al gon kins	An til les
A bac' o	Al kan sas	An to ni o
A bit i bis	A me lia	A pu ri ma
A ca di a	A me ni a	A quid nec
A quac nac	An co cus	Ash cut ney
A las ka	A run del	As sin i boils

An Easy Standard of Pronunciation.

As sump tion
Au re li us
Au ro ra

B

Bald ea gle
Bal div i a
Ba leze
Bark ham sted
Bar thol o mew
Bei laire
Bell grove
Bel pre
Ber bice
Ber mu da
Ber tie
Bil ler i ca
Bo quet
Bos caw en
Brook ha ven

C

Ca bar rus
Co han sie
Ca ho ki a
Ca mil lus
Cam peach y
Caer nar von
Co nan i cut
Ca rac us
Ca ran gas
Car lisle
Cas tine
Ca taw ba
Ca val lo
Cay lo ma
Cay enne
Caz no vi a
Cham blee
Char lo tia

Che buc to
Che mung
Che raws
Chi a pa
Chop tank
Chow an
Cier mont
Chic kau go
Co do rus
Co chel mus
Co col i co
Co che co
Cock sa kie
Co hoc sink
Co han zy
Co has set
Co hoze
Cole rain
Co lum bi a
Co ne sus
Con noc ton
Co hos
Coo saw
Cor dil le ras
Corn wal lis
Coo dras
Cow e tas
Cu ma na

D

Daw fus ky
De fi ance
De troit
Din wid die
Do min go
Du anes burg
Dum fries
Dun bar ton

Du page
Du plin

E

E liz a beth
E liz a beth town
Em ma us
Eu phra ta
Es cam bi a
Eu sta tia
E so pus
Ex u ma

F

Fair ha ven
Fay ette
Fitz will iam
Flat bush
Flu van na

G

Ge ne va
Ge rards town
Go naives
Gwyn nedd
Graves end
Green bush
Guild hall

H

Ha van na
Hel e na
Hen lo pen
Hi was see
Hon du ras

J

Jac mel
Je ru sa lem

An Easy Standard of Pronunciation.

K

Kas kas ki a
Kow sa ki
Key wa wa
Kil lis ti noe
Kil ken ny
King sess ing
Kin sale
Kas kas kunk

L

La com ic
La co ni a
La goon
Le noir
Long bay
Long i sland
Long lake
Long mead ow
Lo ren zo
Lo ret to
Lou i sa
Low hill
Lu cay a
Lu cia
Lu zerne
Ly com ing
Lynn ha ven
Ly san der

M

Ma chi as
Ma cun gy
Ma con nels burg
Ma de ra
Ma hack a mac
Ma ho ney
Ma hone
Ma ho ning

Ma nal lin
Man hat tan
Ma nil lon
Ma quoit
Mar cel lus
Mar gal la way
Ma tane
Ma tan zas
Ma til da
Ma tin i cus
Mat tap o ny
Me dun cook
Me her rin
Mem ram cook
Men do za
Men ol o pen
Me thu en
Mi am i
Mis sisk o
Mine head
Mo bill
Mo he gan
Mo hic con
Mo nad noc
Mon he gan
Mo noc a sy
Mon seag
Mon tauk
Mon te go
Mont gom e ry
Mont pe lier
Mont ville
Mo rant
Mor gan za
Mo shan non
Mul he gan
Musk ing um

N

Na hant
Na mask et
Nan task et
Nan tuck et
Nan tux et
Na shon
Nas keag
Na varre
Ne pon set
Ne sham o ny*
New cas tle
New Eng land
New fane
New paltz
New Roch elle
New U trecht
Ni ag a ra
Ni pis sing
North amp ton
North cas tle
North east
North um ber land

O

Oak fus ky
Oak mul gee
O co ny
O nei da
Or chil la
Os we go
Ot se go
O was co
O we go
O wy hee

P

Pal my ra

* Pronounced Shammony.

An Easy Standard of Pronunciation.

Pa mun ky
Pa nu co
Pa rai ba
Pas sump sic
Pa taps co
Pa tuck et
Pa tux et
Pau tuck et
Pau tux et
Pe gun noc
Pe jep scot
Pe quon uc
Per a mus
Per cip a ny
Per nam bu co
Perth am boy
Phi lop o lis
Py an'ke tunk
Py an ke shaws
Pier mont
Pin chin a
Pi o ri as
Pla cen tia
Po kon ca
Po soom suc
Port roy al
Port penn
Po to si
Pough keep sie
Pound ridge
Presque ile
Pre sums cot
Pro tect worth

Q

Quam pea gan

R

Red hook

Re ho both
Ri van na
Rock on ca ma
Ros seau
Ro siers
Row an

S

Sag har bor
Salt ash
San dus ky
Sa rec to
Sa vil la
Sa voy
Sco har rie
Scow he gan
Se kon net
Se ba go
Sa bas ti cook
Se bas tian
Sem pro ni us
Se wee
Sha wan gunk*
Shaw sheen
She nan go
She tuck et
Sche nec ta dy
Skip pac
South amp ton
South hold
Stra bane
Swan na no
Swa ta ra

T

Tap pan
Ta ba go
Ta bas co
Ta con net

Ta doo sac
Ta en sa
Tar pau lin
Ta wan dy
Ta wixt wy
Ti o ga
To mis ca ning
Tor bay
To ron to
Tor tu gas
Tou lon
Tre coth ic
Trux il lo
Tunk han noc
Ty bee
Ty rone

U

U lys ses
Ur ban na

V

Ver gennes
Ver sailles
Ve nan go

W

Wa cho vi a
Wa chu set
Wal hold ing
Wap pac a mo
Wa tau ga
Wa keag
Web ham et
West chest er
West hamp ton
West In dies
West point
Wi com i co

* Pronounced Shongum.

An Easy Standard of Pronunciation.

Wi mac o mac	Wi nee	Wis cas set
Win eask	Win yaw	Wy o ming

The following have the accent on the third syllable, and most of them a secondary accent on the first.

A
Ab be ville'
Ac a pul co
Ac co mac
Ag a men tic us
Ag a mun tic
Al a bam a
Al a chu a
Al be marl
Al le mand
Al va ra do
Am a zo ni a
Am o noo suc
Am us keag
An ah uac
An as ta sia
An ti cos ti
Ap a lach i an
Ap a lach es
Ap o quen e my
Ap po mat ox
A que doch ton
Arch i pel a go
Au gus tine

B
Bas ken ridge
Bel vi dere
Bag a duce
Beth a ba ra
Bux a loons

C
ner may e

Cagh ne wa ga
Cal e do ni a
Can an dai gua
Can a wisk
Can i co de o
Car ib bee
Car i coo
Car i boo
Car tha ge na
Cat a ra qua
Cat a wis sa
Cat te hunk
Chab a quid ic
Char le mont
Chat a ho chy
Chat a nu ga
Cher o kee
Chet i ma chas
Chic ca mog ga
Chick a hom i ny
Chick a ma ges
Chick a saw
Chil ho wee
Chil i co the
Chil lis quac
Chim bo ra zo
Chris ti an a
Clar e mont
Cin cin na tus
Con a wa go
Con a wan go
Con dus keag
Con e dog we net
C.. .. manga

Cock a la mus
Con es te o
Con es to go
Con ga ree
Coo sa hatch y
Co to pax i
Cur ri tuc
Cus co wil la
Cus se wa ga

D
Dem a ra ra
Des e a da

E
Eb en e zer
En o ree
Es ca ta ri
Es se que bo

F
Fron ti nac
Freid en huet ten

G
Gal li op o lis
Gen ne see
Gen e vieve
Grad en huet ten

I
In di an a

K
Kar a tunk
Kas k. nom pa

An Easy Standard of Pronunciation.

Kay da ros so ra
Ken ne bank
Kick a poo
Kin der hook
is ke man i tas
it ta ning
Kit ta tin ny

L

Lach a wan na
Lech a wax en
Let ter ken ny
Lit tle comp ton

M

Mach a noy
Mag da le na
Mag e gad a vie
Ma gel lan
Ma gel la ni a
Mar a cai bo
Man a han
Mar ble head
Mar cus hook
Mar ga ret ta
Ma ri et ta
Mas sa nu ten
Mau re pas
Mel a was ka
Mem fre ma gog
Mack i naw*
Mi ro goane
Mis sin abe
Mis si quash
Mo hon ton go
Mo non ga lia
Mont re al
Mor ris se na
Moy a men sing

Mus ko gee

N

Na hun keag
Nan se mond
Nau do wes sy
Nic a ra gua
Nip e gon
Niv er nois
Nock a mix on
Nol a chuc ky

O

Oc co chap po
Oc co neach y
Oc co quan
Oc ta ra ro
On a lash ka
Os sa baw
Os we gach y
Ot o gam ics

P

Pak a nok it
Pan a ma
Pan i mar i bo
Pas ca go la
Pas quo tank
Pas sy unk
Pat a go ni a
Pem a quid
Pen sa co la
Per qui mins
Per ki o men
Pitts syl va ni a
Pluck e min
Po ca hon tas
Po co moke
Pont char train
Por to bel lo

Port to bac co
Pot ta wot a mies

Q

Quem a ho ning

R

Reg o lets
Riv er head
Rock e mo ko

S

Sag a mond
Sag a naum
Sag en da go
Sal va dore
Sar a nac
Sar a to ga
Sax e go tha
Scat e cook
Seb a cook
Sem i noles
Sin e pux ent
Scan e at e tes
Soc an da ga
Spot syl va ni a
Sur i nam

T

Tal la see
Tal a poo sy
Tap pa han noc
The a kik i
Tib e ron
Tow a men sing
To ne wan to
To to wa
Tuck a hoc
Tu cu man

* The popular pronunciation of Mishillimackanack.

An Easy Standard of Pronunciation.

Tul pe hock en	W	Wy a lux ing
Tus ca ro ra	Wah que tank	Wy o noke
U	Wil li man tic	Y
U na dil la	Win ne ba go	Yu ca tan
Vi nal ha ven	Wy a lu sing	Yoh o ga ny

The following are accented on the fourth syllable.

Can a jo har ry	Mo non ga he la
Can a se ra ga	Om pom pa noo suc
Can e de ra go	Pas sam a quod dy
Chick a ma com i co	Pem i ge was set
Cob bes e con ty	Quin sig a mond
Co hon go ron to	Rip pa ca noe
Cou e go cheag	Sag a da hoc
Dam e ris cot ta	Sax a pa haw
Eas tan al lee	Ti con de ro ga
Kish a co quil las	Wa nas pe tuck et
Mish il li mack a nack*	

* Pronounced, Mackinaw.

Islands of the West Indies.

An guil' la	Por to ri' co§	Ne vis
An ti' gua*	Eu sta tia	To' ba go
Ba ha ma	Gre na da	Trin i dad'
Ber mu' da	Gua da lou'pe‖	Sant a Cru'se
Bar ba' does	Hay ti or	St. Christ' o phers
Bar bu' da	His pan i o' la	St. Lu' cia¶
Cur a so'	Ja ma'i ca	St. Mar tins
Cu' ba	Mar i ga lant'	St. Thom as
Dom in i' co†	Miq ue lon	St. Vin cent
Mar tin i' co‡	Mont ser rat'	

---

* Pronounced, Antega.	† Domineke.	‡ Martineke.
§ Portoreko.	‖ Gaudaloop	¶ Saint Luzee

An Easy Standard of Pronunciation.

TABLE LII.

OF NUMBERS.

Figures.	Letters.	Names	Numerical Adjectives.
1	I	one	first
2	II	two	second
3	III	three	third
4	IV	four	fourth
5	V	five	fifth
6	VI	six	sixth
7	VII	seven	seventh
8	VIII	eight	eighth
9	IX	nine	ninth
10	X	ten	tenth
11	XI	eleven	eleventh
12	XII	twelve	twelfth
13	XIII	thirteen	thirteenth
14	XIV	fourteen	fourteenth
15	XV	fifteen	fifteenth
16	XVI	sixteen	sixteenth
17	XVII	seventéen	seventeenth
18	XVIII	eighteen	eighteenth
19	XIX	nineteen	nineteenth
20	XX	twenty	twentieth
30	XXX	thirty	thirtieth
40	XL	forty	fortieth
50	L	fifty	fiftieth
60	LX	sixty	sixtieth
70	LXX	seventy	seventieth
80	LXXX	eighty	eightieth
90	XC	ninety	ninetieth
100	C	one hundred	one hundredth
200	CC	two hundred	two hundredth
300	CCC	three hundred	three hundredth
400	CCCC	four hundred	four hundredth
500	D	five hundred	five hundredth
600	DC	six hundred	six hundredth
700	DCC	seven hundred	seven hundredth
800	DCCC	eight hundred	eight hundredth
900	DCCCC	nine hundred	nine hundredth
1000	M	one thousand, &c.	one thousandth
1827	MDCCCXXVII	one thousand eight-hundred and twenty-seven.	

An Easy Standard of Pronunciation.

TABLE LIII.

Words of the same sound, but different in spelling and signification.

AIL, to be troubled
Ale, malt liquor
Air, an element
Are, plural of is or am
Heir, to an estate
All, the whole
Awl, an instrument
Al tar, for sacrifice
Al ter, to change
Ant, a pismire
Aunt, uncle's wife
As cent, steepness
As sent, an agreement
Au ger, an instrument
Au gur, one who foretells
Bail, surety
Bale, a pack of goods
Ball, a round substance
Bawl, to cry aloud
Bare, naked
Bear, to suffer
Bear, a beast
Base, vile
Bass, in music
Beer, a liquor
Bier, to carry the dead
Ber ry, a small fruit
Bu ry, to inter the dead
Beat, to strike
Beet, a root
Blew, did blow
Blue, color
Boar, a male swine
Bore, to make a hole
Bow, to bend
Bough, a branch

Bow, to shoot with
Beau, a gay fellow
Bred, brought up
Bread, food
Bur row, for rabbits
Bo rough, a town corpo-
    rate
By, a particle
Buy, to purchase
Cain, a man's name
Cane, a shrub, or staff
Call, to cry out
Caul, of a wig or bowels
Can non, a large gun
Can on, a rule
Can vass, to examine
Can vas, coarse cloth
Ceil ing, of a room
Seal ing, setting of a seal
Cell, a hut
Sell, to dispose of
Cen tu ry, a hundred
    years
Cen tau ry, an herb
Chol er, wrath
Col lar, for the neck
Cord, a small rope
Chord, in music
Ci on, a young shoot
Si on, a mountain
Cite, to summon
Sight, seeing
Site, situation
Chron i cal, of a long con-
    tinuance
Chron i cle, a history

An Easy Standard of Pronunciation.

Co rse, order or direction
Coarse, not fine
Com ple ment, a full num-
 ber
Com pli ment, expression
 of civility
Cous in, a relation
Coz en, to cheat
Coun cil, an assembly
Coun sel, advice
Cur rant, a berry
Cur rent, passing, or a
 stream
Deer, a wild animal
Dear, of great price
Dew, from heaven
Due, owed
Die, to expire
Dye, to color
Doe, a female deer
Dough, bread unbaked
Dun, brown color
Done, performed
Fane, a weathercock
Fain, gladly
Feign, to dissemble
Faint, weary
Feint, a false march
Fair, comely
Fare, food, customary
 duty, &c.
Fel on, a whitlow
Fel on, a criminal
Flea, an insect
Flee, to run away
Flour, of wheat
Flow er, of the field
Fourth, in number
Forth, abroad

Foul, nasty
Fowl, a bird
Gilt, with gold
Guilt, crime
Grate, for coals
Great, large
Groan, to sigh
Grown, increased
Hail, to salute, or frozen
 drops of rain
Hale, sound, healthy
Hart, a beast
Heart, the seat of life
Hare, an animal
Hair, of the head
Here, in this place
Hear, to hearken
Hew, to cut
Hue, color
Him, that man
Hymn, a sacred song
Hire, wages
High er, more high
Heel, of the foot
Heal, to cure
I, myself
Eye, organ of sight
Isle, an island
Ile, of a church
In, within
Inn, a tavern
In dite, to compose
In dict, to prosecute
Kill, to slay
Kiln, of brick
Knave, a dishonest man
Nave, of a wheel
Knight, by honor
Night, the evening

An Easy Standard of Pronunciation.

Know, to be acquainted
No, not so
Knew, did know
New, not old
Knot, made by tying
Not, denying
Lade, to dip water
Laid, placed
Lain, did lie
Lane, a narrow passage
Leek, a root
Leak, to run out
Les son, a reading
Les sen, to diminish
Li ar, a teller of lies
Lyre, a harp
Led, did lead
Lead, heavy metal
Lie, a falsehood, also to rest on a bed
Lye, water drained through ashes
Lo, behold
Low, humble
Made, finished
Maid, an unmarried woman
Main, the chief
Mane, of a horse
Male, the he kind
Mail, armor, or a packet
Man ner, mode or custom
Man or, a lordship
Meet, to come together
Meat, flesh
Mete, measure
Mite, an insect
Might, strength
Met al, gold, silver, &c.
Met tle, briskness

Naught, bad
Nought, none
Nay, no
Neigh, as a horse
Oar, to row with
Ore, metal not separated
Oh, alas
Owe, to be indebted
One, in number
Won, past time of *win*
Our, belonging
Hour, sixty minutes
Pale, wanting color
Pail, a vessel
Pain, torment
Pane, a square of glass
Peel, the outside
Peal, upon the bells
Pear, a fruit
Pare, to cut off
Plain, even, or level
Plain, to make smooth
Plate, a flat piece of metal
Plait, a fold in a garment
Pray, to implore
Prey, a booty
Prin ci pal, chief
Prin ci ple, first rule
Proph et, a foreteller
Prof it, advantage
Peace, tranquillity
Piece, a part
Rain, falling water
Rein, of a bridle
Reign, to rule
Reed, a shrub
Read, to peruse
Rest, ease
Wrest, to force

An Easy Standard of Pronunciation.

Rice, a sort of corn
Rise, origin
  Rye, a sort of grain
  Wry, crooked
Ring, to sound
Wring, to twist
  Rite, ceremony
  Right, just
Write, to form letters with
  a pen
Wright, a workman
  Rode, did ride
  Road, the highway
Roe, a deer
Row, a rank
  Ruff, a neckcloth
  Rough, not smooth
Sail, of a ship
Sale, a selling
  Seen, beheld
  Scene, of a stage
See, to behold
Sea, the ocean
  Sent, ordered away
  Scent, smell
Sen ior, elder
Seign or, a lord
  Shore, side of a river
  Shoar, a prop
Sink, to go down
Cinque, five
  So, thus
  Sow, to scatter
Sum, the whole
Some, a part
  Sun, the fountain of light
  Son, a male child
Sore, an ulcer
Soar, to mount up

Stare, to look earnestly
Stair, a step
Steel, hard metal
Steal, to take without lib-
  erty
Suc cor, help
Suck er, a young twig
Sleight, dexterity
Slight, to despise
  Sole, of the foot
  Soul, the spirit
Tax, a rate
Tacks, small nails
  Tale, a story
  Tail, the end
Tare, weight allowed
Tear, to rend
  Team, of cattle or horses
  Teem, to go with young
Their, belonging to them
There, in that place
  The, a particle
  Thee, yourself
Too, likewise
Two, twice one
  Tow, to drag after
  Toe, of the foot
Vale, a valley
Veil, a covering
  Vein, for the blood
  Vane, to show the course
    of the wind
Vice, sin
Vise, a screw
  Wait, to tarry
  Weight, heaviness
Wear, to put on
Ware, merchandize
Were, past time plu. of am

An Easy Standard of Pronunciation.

Waste, to spend
Waist, the middle
Way, road
Weigh, to poise
Week, seven days
Weak, not strong

Wood, trees
Would, was willing
You, plural of we
Yew, a tree

TABLE LIV.
Of ABBREVIATIONS.

A. A. S. Fellow of the American Academy

C. A. S. Fellow of the Connecticut Academy

A. B. Bachelor of Arts

A. D. In the year of our Lord

A. M. Master of Arts, before noon, or in the year of the world

Bart. Baronet

B. D. Bachelor of Divinity

C. or Cent. an hundred

Capt. Captain

Col. Colonel

Cant. Canticles

Chap. Chapter

Chron. Chronicles

Co. Company

Com. Commissioner

Cr. Credit

Cwt. Hundred weight

D. D. Doctor of Divinity

Dr. Doctor or Debtor

Dec. December

Dep. Deputy

Deut. Deuteronomy

Do. or ditto, the same

E. G. for example

Ecclesiastes

Ep. Epistl

Eng. English

Eph. Ephesians

Esa. Esaias

Ex. Example, or Exodus

Feb. February

Fr. France, or Francis

F. R. S. Fellow of the Royal Society

Gal. Galatians

Gen. Genesis

Gent. Gentleman

Geo. George

G. R. George the King

Heb. Hebrews

Hon. Honorable

Hund. Hundred

Ibidem, ibid. In the same place

Isa. Isaiah

i. e. that is

Id. the same

Jan. January

Ja. James

Jac. Jacob

Josh. Joshua

K. King

Km. Kingdom

Kt. Knight

L. Lord or Lady

An Easy Standard of Pronunciation.

Lev. Leviticus	P. S. Postscript
Lieut. Lieutenant	Ps. Psalm
L. L. D. Doctor of Laws	Q. Question, Queen
L. S. the place of the Seal	q. d. as if he should say
Lond. London	q. l. as much as you please
M. Marquis	Regr. Register
M. B. Bachelor of Physic	Rev. Revelation, Reverend
M. D. Doctor of Physic	Rt. Hon. Right Honorable
Mr. Master	S. South and Shilling
Messrs. Gentlemen, Sirs	St. Saint
Mrs. Mistress	Sept. September
M. S. Manuscript	Serj. Serjeant
M. S. S. Manuscripts	S. T. P. Professor of Divin
Mat. Matthew	ity
Math. Mathematics	S. T. D. Doctor of Divinit
N. B. take particular notice	ss. to wit, namely
Nov. November	Theo. Theophilus
No. Number	Tho. Thomas
N. S. New Style	Thess. Thessalonians
Obj. Objection	V. or vide, see
Oct. October	Viz. to wit, namely
O. S. Old Style	Wm. William
Parl. Parliament	Wp. Worship
Per cent. by the hundred	&. and
Pet. Peter	&c. and so forth
Phil. Philip	U. S. A. United States o
Philom. a lover of learning	America
P. M. Afternoon	

EXPLANATION

Of the Pauses and other Characters used in Writing.

A Comma (,) is a pause of one syllable— semicolon (;) two —A colon (:) four—A period (.) six—An interrogation point (?) shows when a question is asked; as, *What do you see?*—An exclamation point (!) is a mark of wonder or surprise; as, *O the folly of sinners!*—The pause of these two points is the same as a colon or a period, and the sentence should usually be closed with a raised tone of voice.

( ) A Parenthesis includes a part of a sentence, which is not necessary to make sense, and should be read quicker, and in a weaker tone of voice.

An Easy Standard of Pronunciation.

[ ] Brackets or Hooks, include words that serve to explain a foregoing word or sentence.

- A Hyphen joins words or syllables; as, *sea-water.*

' An Apostrophe shows when a letter is omitted, as, *us'd* for used.

ʌ A Caret shows when a word or number of words are omitted through mistake; as, *this is* ^*my* *book.*

" A quotation, or double comma, includes a passage that is taken from some other author in his own words.

☞ The Index points to some remarkable passage.

¶ The Paragraph begins a new subject.

§ The Section is used to divide chapters.

*†‡‖ An Asterisk, and other references, point to a note in the margin, or bottom of a page.

OF CAPITAL LETTERS.

Sentences should begin with a capital letter—also every line in poetry. Proper names, which are the names of persons, places, rivers, mountains, lakes, &c. should begin with a capital. Also, the name of the Supreme Being.

ADDITIONAL LESSONS.

DOMESTIC ECONOMY,

Or, the History of Thrifty and Unthrifty.

THERE is a great difference among men, in their ability to gain property; but a still greater difference in their power of using it to advantage. Two men may acquire the same amount of money, in a given time; yet one will prove to be a poor man, while the other becomes rich. A chief and essential difference in the management of property, is, that one man spends only the *interest* of his money, while another spends the *principal.*

I know a farmer by the name of Thrifty, who manages his affairs in this manner: He rises early in the morning, looks to the condition of his house, barn, home-lot and stock—sees that his cattle, horses and hogs are fed; examines the tools to see whether they are all in good order for the workmen—takes care that breakfast is ready in due season, and begins work in the cool of

the day—When in the field, he keeps steadily at work,
though not so violently as to fatigue and exhaust the
body—nor does he stop to tell or hear long stories—
When the labor of the day is past, he takes refreshment,
and goes to rest at an early hour—In this manner he
earns and gains money.

When *Thrifty* has acquired a little property, he does
not spend it or let it slip from him, without use or bene-
fit. He pays his taxes and debts when due or called for,
so that he has no officers' fees to pay, nor expenses of
courts. He does not frequent the tavern, and drink up
all his earnings in liquor that does him no good. He
puts his money to use, that is, he buys more land, or
stock, or lends his money at interest—in short, he makes
his money produce some profit or income. These sav-
ings and profits, though small by themselves, amount in
a year to a considerable sum, and in a few years they
swell to an estate—Thrifty becomes a wealthy farmer,
with several hundred acres of land, and a hundred head
of cattle.

Very different is the management of UNTHRIFTY: He
lies in bed till a late hour in the morning—then rises,
and goes to the bottle for a dram, or to the tavern for a
glass of bitters—Thus he spends six cents before breakfast, for a dram that makes him dull and heavy all day.
He gets his breakfast late, when he ought to be at work.
When he supposes he is ready to begin the work of
the day, he finds he has not the necessary tools, or some
of them are out of order,—the plow-share is to be sent
half a mile to a blacksmith to be mended ; a tooth or
two in a rake or the handle of a hoe is broke ; or a sythe
or an ax is to be ground.—Now, he is in a great hurry,
he bustles about to make preparation for work—and
what is done in a hurry is ill done—he loses a part of
the day in getting ready—and perhaps the time of his
workmen. At ten or eleven o'clock, he is ready to go
to work—then comes a boy and tells him, the sheep have
escaped from the pasture—or the cows have got among
his corn—or the hogs into the garden—He frets and

An Easy Standard of Pronunciation.

storms, and runs to drive them out—a half hour or more time is lost in driving the cattle from mischief, and repairing a poor old broken fence—a fence that answers no purpose but to lull him into security, and teach his horses and cattle to be unruly—After all this bustle, the fatigue of which is worse than common labor, *Unthrifty* is ready to begin a day's work at twelve o'clock.—Thus half his time is lost in supplying defects, which proceed from want of foresight and good management. His small crops are damaged or destroyed by unruly cattle. —His barn is open and leaky, and what little he gathers, is injured by the rain and snow.—His house is in a like condition—the shingles and clapboards fall off and let in the water, which causes the timber, floors and furniture to decay—and exposed to inclemencies of weather, his wife and children fall sick—their time is lost, and the mischief closes with a ruinous train of expenses for medicines and physicians.—After dragging out some years of disappointment, misery and poverty, the lawyer and the sheriff sweep away the scanty remains of his estate. This is the history of UNTHRIFTY—his principal is spent —he has no interest.

Not unlike this, is the history of the Grog-drinker. This man wonders why he does not thrive in the world ; he cannot see the reason why his neighbor *Temperance* should be more prosperous than himself—but in truth, he makes no calculations. Ten cents a day for grog, is a small sum, he thinks, which can hurt no man ! But let us make an estimate—arithmetic is very useful for a man who ventures to spend small sums every day. Ten cents a day amount in a year to thirty-six dollars and a half—a sum sufficient to buy a good farm-horse ! This surely is no small sum for a farmer or mechanic—But in ten years, this sum amounts to three hundred and sixty-five dollars, besides interest in the mean time ! What an amount is this for drams and bitters in ten years ! it is money enough to build a small house ! But look at the amount in thirty years !—One thousand and ninety-five dollars !—What a vast sum to run down one man's throat

An Easy Standard of Pronunciation.

in liquor—a sum that will buy a farm sufficient to main-
tain a small family. Suppose a family to consume a
quart of spirits in a day, at twenty-five cents a quart.
The amount of this in a year, is ninety-one dollars and a
quarter—in ten years, nine hundred and twelve dollars
and a half—and in thirty years, two thousand seven hundred and thirty-seven dollars and a half! A great estate may be thus consumed, in single quarts of rum! What
mischief is done by the love of spirituous liquors!

But, says the laboring man, " I cannot work without
spirits—I must have something to give me strength."
Then drink something that will give durable nourishment
—Of all the substances taken into the stomach, spirituous
liquors contain the least nutriment, and add the least to
bodily vigor. Malt liquors, molasses and water, milk and
water, contain nutriment, and even cider is not wholly
destitute of it—but distilled spirituous liquors contain
little or none.

But, says the laborer or the traveller, " spirituous liquors
warm the stomach, and are very useful in cold weather"—
No, this is not correct. Spirits enliven the feelings for half
an hour—but leave the body more dull, languid and cold
than it was before. A man will freeze the sooner for
drinking spirits of any kind. If a man wishes to guard
against cold, let him eat a biscuit, a bit of bread, or a
meal of victuals. Four ounces of bread will give a more
durable warmth to the body, than a gallon of spirits—food
is the natural stimulant or exciting power of the human
body—it gives warmth and strength, and does not leave
the body, as spirit does, more feeble and languid.—The
practice of drinking spirits gives a man red eyes, a bloat-
ed face, and an empty purse—It injures the liver, pro-
duces dropsy, occasions a trembling of the joints and
limbs, and closes life with a slow decay or palsy—This
is a short history of the drinker of distilled spirits. If a
few drinking men are found to be exceptions to this account, still the remarks are true, as they apply to most
cases. Spirituous liquors shorten more lives than famine,
pestilence, and the sword!

An Easy Standard of Pronunciation.

LESSONS ON FAMILIAR SUBJECTS.

All mankind live on the fruits of the earth—the first and most necessary employment, therefore, is the tillage of the ground, called agriculture, husbandry, or farming. The farmer clears his land of trees, roots and stones—he surrounds it with a fence of poles, posts and rails, stone wall, hedge or ditch. He plows and harrows, or drags the soil, to break the clods or turf, and make it mellow and pliable—he manures it also, if necessary, with stable dung, ashes, marl, plaster, lime, sea-shells, or decayed vegetable substances. He plants maiz in rows, or sows wheat, barley, rye, oats, buckwheat, flax or hemp. He hoes the maiz two or three times, kills the weeds, and draws the earth round the hills to support and nourish the plants.—When the grain is ripe, he reaps or cradles his grain, and pulls the flax.—The ears of maiz are picked by hand, or the stalks cut with a sickle or knife, and the husks are stripped off in the evening. With what joy does the farmer gather his crops of the former and latter harvest!—He toils indeed, but he reaps the fruit of his labor in peace—he fills his granary in summer, and in autumn presents a thank-offering to God for his bounty.

See the mower, how he swings his sythe!—The grass falls prostrate before him—the glory of the field is laid low—the land is stripped of its verdant covering. See the stripling follow his father or brother, and with a pitchfork, spread the thick swath, and shake the grass about the meadow! How fragrant the smell of new made hay—how delightful the task to tend it!

Enter the forest of the wilderness; see here and there a rustic dwelling made of logs; a little spot cleared and cultivated; a thatched hovel to shelter a cow and her food; the forest resounding with the ax-man's blows, as he levels the sturdy beach, maple, or hemlock; while the crackling fire aids his hands, by consuming the massy piles of wood which he cannot remove; hear the howling wolf, or watch the nimble deer, as he bounds along among the trees; the faithful cow, in search of shrubs

An Easy Standard of Pronunciation.

and twigs, strays from the cottage, and the owner seeks her at evening, in the gloomy forest; led by the tinkling of the bell, he finds and drives her home. A bowl of bread and milk furnishes him with his frugal repast; he retires weary to rest—and the sleep of the laboring man is sweet.

See the dairy woman, while she fills her pails with new milk—the gentle cows quietly chewing their cuds by her side. Enter the milk-room, see the pans, pails and tubs, how clean and sweet, all in order, and fit for use! The milk strained and put in a cool place—the cream skimmed off for butter, or the milk set for cheese—Here is a churn as white as ivory—there a cheese-press forcing the whey from the curd! See the shelves filled with cheeses—what a noble sight! and butter as yellow as the purest gold!

George, let us look into the work-shops among the mechanics. Here is a carpenter, he squares a post or a beam; he scores or notches it first, and then hews it with his broad-ax. He bores holes with an auger, and with the help of a chisel, forms a mortise for a tenon. He measures with a square or rule, and marks his work with a compass. Each timber is fitted to its place. The sills support the posts, and these support the beams. Braces secure the frame of a building from swaying or leaning—Girders and joists support the floors; studs, with the posts, support the walls, and rafters uphold the roof.

Now comes the joiner with his chest of tools. He planes the boards, joints the shingles, and covers the building—With his saw he cuts boards, with his gimblet or wimble, he makes holes for nails, pins or spikes—with his chisel and gouge, he makes mortises.

Then comes the mason with his trowel—the laths are nailed to the studs and joists to support the plaster; first a rough coat of coarse mortar of lime and sand is laid on, and this is covered with a beautiful white plaster. And last of all comes the painter with his brush and oil-pots—he mixes the oil and white lead, and gives to the apartments the color which the owner or his lady sees fit to direct.

An Easy Standard of Pronunciation.

A MORAL CATECHISM.

Question. WHAT is moral virtue?

Answer. It is an honest, upright conduct in all our dealings with men.

Q. What rules have we to direct us in our moral conduct?

A. God's word, contained in the bible, has furnished all necessary rules to direct our conduct.

Q. In what part of the bible are these rules to be found?

A. In almost every part : but the most important duties between men are summed up in the beginning of Matthew, in CHRIST's Sermon on the Mount.

OF HUMILITY.

Q. What is humility?

A. A lowly temper of mind.

Q. What are the advantages of humility?

A. The advantages of humility in this life are very numerous and great. The humble man has few or no enemies. Every one loves him, and is ready to do him good. If he is rich and prosperous, people do not envy him ; if he is poor and unfortunate, every one pities him, and is disposed to alleviate his distresses.

Q. What is pride?

A. A lofty high-minded disposition.

Q. Is pride commendable?

A. By no means. A modest, self-approving opinion of our own good deeds is very right—it is natural—it is agreeable, and a spur to good actions. But we should not suffer our hearts to be blown up with pride, whatever great and good deeds we have done; for pride brings upon us the ill-will of mankind, and displeasure of our Maker.

Q. What effect has humility upon our own minds?

A. Humility is attended with peace of mind and self-satisfaction. The humble man is not disturbed with cross accidents, and is never fretful and uneasy ; nor does he repine when others grow rich. He is contented, because his mind is at ease.

Q: What is the effect of pride on a man's happiness?

A. Pride exposes a man to numberless disappoint-

An Easy Standard of Pronunciation.

ments and mortifications. The proud man expects more attention and respect will be paid to him, than he deserves, or than others are willing to pay him. He is neglected, laughed at and despised, and this treatment frets him, so that his own mind becomes a seat of torment. A proud man cannot be a happy man.

Q. What has Christ said respecting the virtue of humility?

A. He has said, " Blessed are the poor in spirit, for theirs is the kingdom of heaven." Poorness of spirit is humility ; and this humble temper prepares a man for heaven, where all is peace and love.

OF MERCY.

Q. What is mercy?

A. It is tenderness of heart.

Q. What are the advantages of this virtue?

A. The exercise of it tends to diffuse happiness and lessen the evils of life. Rulers of a merciful temper will make their *good* subjects happy ; and will not torment the *bad* with needless severity. Parents and masters will not abuse their children and servants with harsh treatment. More love, more confidence, more happiness, will subsist among men, and of course society will be happier.

Q. Should not beasts as well as men be treated with mercy?

A. They ought indeed. It is wrong to give needless pain even to a beast. Cruelty to the brutes shows a man has a hard heart, and if a man is unfeeling to a beast, he will not have much feeling for men. If a man treats his beast with cruelty, beware of trusting yourself in his power. He will probably make a severe master and a cruel husband.

Q. How does cruelty show its effects?

A. A cruel disposition is usually exercised upon those who are under its power. Cruel rulers make severe laws, which injure the persons and properties of their subjects. Cruel officers execute laws in a severe manner, when it is not necessary for public good. A cruel husband abuses his wife and children. A cruel master acts the tyrant over his apprentices and servants. The effects of cruelty are, hatred, quarrels, tumults and wretchedness.

An Easy Standard of Pronunciation.

Q. What does Christ say of the merciful man?

A. He says he is " blessed, for he shall obtain mercy." He who shows mercy and tenderness to others, will be treated with tenderness and compassion himself.

OF PEACE-MAKERS.

Q. Who are peace-makers?

A. All who endeavor to prevent quarrels and disputes among men ; or to reconcile those who are separated by strife.

Q. Is it unlawful to contend with others on any occasion?

A. It is impossible to avoid some differences with men ; but disputes should be always conducted with temper and moderation. The man who keeps his temper will not be rash, and do or say things which he will afterwards repent of. And though men should sometimes differ, still they should be friends. They should be ready to do kind offices to each other.

Q. What is the reward of the peace-maker?

A. He shall be " blessed, and called the child of God." The mild, peaceable, friendly man, resembles God. What an amiable character is this ! To be like our heavenly Father, that lovely, perfect and glorious being, who is the source of all good, is to be the best and happiest of men.

OF PURITY OF HEART.

Q. What is a pure heart?

A. A heart free from all bad desires, and inclined to conform to the divine will in all things.

Q. Should a man's intentions as well as his actions be good?

A. Most certainly. Actions cannot be called *good,* unless they proceed from good motives. We should wish to see and make all men better and happier—we should rejoice at their prosperity. This is benevolence.

Q. What reward is promised to the pure in heart?

A. Christ has declared " they shall see God." A pure heart is like God, and those who possess it shall dwell in his presence and enjoy his favor forever.

OF ANGER.

Q. Is it right ever to be angry?

An Easy Standard of Pronunciation.

A. It is right in certain cases that we should be angry ; as when gross affronts are offered to us, and injuries done us by design. A suitable spirit of resentment, in such cases, will obtain justice for us, and protect us from further insults

Q. By what rule should anger be governed ?

A. We should never be angry without cause ; that is, we should be certain that a person *means* to affront, injure or insult us, before we suffer ourselves to be angry. It is wrong, it is mean, it is a mark of a little mind, to take fire at every little trifling dispute. And when we have real cause to be angry, we should observe moderation. We should never be in a passion. A passionate man is like a madman, and is always inexcusable. We should be cool, even in anger ; and be angry no longer than to obtain justice. In short, we should " be angry and sin not."

OF REVENGE.

Q. What is revenge ?

A. It is to injure a man because he has injured us.

Q. Is this justifiable ?

A. Never, in any possible case. Revenge is, perhaps, the meanest as well as wickedest vice in society.

Q. What shall a man do to obtain justice when he is injured ?

A. In general, laws have made provision for doing justice to every man ; and it is right and honorable, when a man is injured, that he should seek a recompence. But a recompence is all he can demand, and of that he should not be his own judge, but should submit the matter to judges appointed by authority.

Q. But suppose a man insults us in such a manner that the law cannot give us redress ?

A. Then forgive him. " If a man strikes you on one cheek, turn the other to him," and let him repeat the abuse, rather than strike him.

Q. But if we are in danger from the blows of another, may we not defend ourselves ?

A. Most certainly. We have always a right to defend our persons, property and families. But we have no right

An Easy Standard of Pronunciation.

to fight and abuse people merely for revenge. 'Tis nobler to forgive. " Love your enemies—bless them that curse you—do good to them that hate you—pray for them that use you ill,"—these are the commands of the blessed Savior of men. The man who does this, is great and good ; he is as much above the little, mean, revengeful man, as virtue is above vice, or as heaven is higher than hell.

OF JUSTICE.

Q. What is justice?

A.   It is giving to every man his due.

Q. Is it always easy to know what is just?

A.   It is generally easy ; and where there is any difficulty in determining, let a man consult the golden rule— " To do to others, what he could reasonably wish they should do to him in the same circumstances."

Q. What are the ill effects of injustice?

A.   If a man does injustice, or rather, if he refuses to do justice, he must be compelled.. Then follows a lawsuit, with a series of expenses, and what is worse, ill-blood and enmity between the parties. Somebody is always the worse for lawsuits, and of course society is less happy.

OF GENEROSITY.

Q. What is generosity?

A.   It is some act of kindness performed for another which strict justice does not demand.

Q. Is this a virtue?

A.   It is indeed a noble virtue. To do justice, is well ; but to do more than justice, is still better, and may proceed from nobler motives.

Q. What has Christ said respecting generosity?

A.   He has commanded us to be generous in this passage, " Whosoever shall compel (or urge) you to go a *mile*, go with him *two*."

Q. Are we to perform this literally?

A.   The meaning of this command will not always require this. But in general we are to do more for others than they ask, provided we can do it without essentially injuring ourselves. We ought cheerfully to suffer many

An Easy Standard of Pronunciation.

inconveniences to oblige others, though we are not required to do ourselves any essential injury.

Q. Of what advantage is generosity to the man who exercises it ?

A. It lays others under obligations to the generous man ; and the probability is, that he will be repaid three fold. Every man on earth wants favors at some time or other in his life ; and if we will not help others, others will not help us. It is for a man's interest to be generous.

Q. Ought we to do kind actions because it is for our interest ?

A. This may be a motive at all times ; but if it is the principal motive, it is less honorable. We ought to do good, as we have opportunity, at all times, and to all men, whether we expect a reward or not ; for if we do good, somebody is the happier for it. This alone is reason enough, why we should do all the good in our power.

OF GRATITUDE.

Q. What is gratitude ?

A. A thankfulness of heart for favors received.

Q. Is it a duty to be thankful for favours?

A. It is a duty and a virtue. A man who does not feel grateful for kind acts done for him by others, does not deserve favors of any kind. He ought to be shut out from the society of the good. He is worse than a savage, for a savage never forgets an act of kindness.

Q. What is the effect of true kindness ?

A. It softens the heart towards the generous man, and every thing which subdues the pride and other unsocial passions of the heart, fits a man to be a better citizen, a better neighbor, a better husband and a better friend. A man who is sensible of favors, and ready to acknowledge them, is more inclined to perform kind offices, not only towards his benefactor, but towards all others.

OF TRUTH.

Q. What is truth ?

A. It is speaking and acting agreeable to fact.

Q. Is it a duty to speak truth at all times ?

A. If we speak at all, we should tell the truth. It is

An Easy Standard of Pronunciation.

not always necessary to tell what we know. There are many things which concern ourselves and others, which we had better not publish to the world.

Q. What rules are there respecting the publishing of truth?

A. 1. When we are called upon to testify in courts, we should speak the whole truth, and that without disguise. To leave out small circumstances, or to give a coloring to others, with a view to favor one side more than the other, is to the highest degree criminal.

2. When we know something of our neighbor which is against his character, we may not publish it, unless to prevent his doing an injury to another person.

3. When we sell any thing to another, we ought not to represent the article to be better than it really is. If there are faults in it which may easily be seen, the law of man does not require us to inform the buyer of these faults, because he may see them himself. But it is not honorable, nor generous, nor strictly honest, to conceal even apparent faults. But when faults are out of sight, the seller ought to tell the buyer of them. If he does not, he is a cheat and a downright knave.

Q. What are the ill effects of lying and deceiving?

A. The man who lies, deceives, or cheats, loses his reputation. No person will believe him, even when he speaks the truth; he is shunned as a pest to society.

Falsehood and cheating destroy all confidence between man and man; they raise jealousies and suspicions among men; they thus weaken the bands of society and destroy happiness. Besides, cheating often strips people of their property, and makes them poor and wretched.

OF CHARITY AND GIVING ALMS.

Q. What is charity?

A. It signifies giving to the poor, or it is a favorable opinion of men and their actions.

Q. When and how far is it our duty to give to the poor?

A. When others really want what we can spare without material injury to ourselves, it is our duty to give them something to relieve their wants.

An Easy Standard of Pronunciation.

Q. When persons are reduced to want by their own laziness and vices, by drunkenness, gambling and the like, is it a duty to relieve them?

A. In general, it is not. The man who gives money and provisions to a lazy, vicious man, becomes a partaker of his guilt. Perhaps it may be right, to give such a man a meal of victuals to keep him from starving, and it is certainly right to feed his wife and family, and make them comfortable.

Q. Who are the proper objects of charity?

A. Persons who are reduced to want by sickness, unavoidable losses by fire, storms at sea or land, drouth, or accidents of other kinds. To such persons we are commanded to give ; and it is our own interest to be charitable ; for we are all liable to misfortunes, and may want charity ourselves.

Q. In what manner should we bestow favors?

A. We should do it with gentleness and affection ; putting on no airs of pride and arrogance. We should also take no pains to publish our charities, but rather to conceal them ; for if we boast of our generosity, we discover that we give from mean, selfish motives. Christ commands us, in giving alms, not to let our left hand know what our right hand doeth.

Q. How can charity be exercised in our opinions of others?

A. By thinking favorably of them and their actions. Every man has his faults ; but charity will not put a harsh construction on another's conduct. It will not charge his conduct to bad views and motives, unless this appears very clear indeed.

OF AVARICE

Q. What is avarice?

A. An excessive desire of possessing wealth.

Q. Is this commendable?

A. It is not ; but one of the meanest of vices.

Q. Can an avaricious man be an honest man?

A. It is hardly possible ; for the lust of gain is almost always accompanied with a disposition to take mean and undue advantages of others.

An Easy Standard of Pronunciation.

Q. What effect has avarice upon the heart?

A. It contracts the heart, narrows the sphere of benevolence, blunts all the fine feelings of sensibility, and sours the mind towards society. An avaricious man, a miser, a niggard, is wrapped up in selfishness, like some worms, which crawl about and eat for some time to fill themselves, then wind themselves up in separate coverings and die.

Q. What injury is done by avarice to society?

A. Avarice gathers together more property than the owner wants, and keeps it hoarded up, where it does no good. The poor are thus deprived of some business, some means of support; the property gains nothing to the community; and somebody is less happy by means of this hoarding of wealth.

Q. In what proportion does avarice do hurt?

A. In an exact proportion to its power of doing good. The miser's *heart* grows *less*, in proportion as his *estate* grows *larger*. The more money he has, the more he has people in his power, and the more he grinds the face of the poor. The larger the tree, and the more spreading the branches, the more small plants are shaded and robbed of their nourishment.

OF FRUGALITY and ECONOMY.

Q. What is the distinction between frugality and avarice?

A. Frugality is a prudent saving of property from needless waste. Avarice gathers more, and spends less than is necessary,

Q. What is economy?

A. It is frugality in expenses—it is a prudent management of one's estate. It disposes of property for useful purposes without waste.

Q. How far does true economy extend?

A. To the saving of every thing which is not necessary to spend for comfort and convenience; and the keeping one's expenses within his income or earnings.

Q. What is wastefulness?

A. It is the spending of money for what is not wanted. If a man drinks a dram which is not necessary for him, buys a cane which he does not want, he wastes his

An Easy Standard of Pronunciation.

money. He injures *himself*, as much as if he had thrown away his money.

Q. Is not waste often occasioned by mere negligence?

A. Very often. The man who does not keep his house and barn well covered ; who does not keep good fences about his fields; who suffers his farming utensils to lie out in the rain on the ground; or his cattle to waste manure in the high way,—is as much a spendthrift as the tavern hunter, the tipler and the gamester.

Q. Do not careless, slovenly people work harder than the neat and orderly?

A. Much harder. It is more labor to destroy a growth of sturdy weeds, than to pull them up when they first spring from the ground. So the disorders and abuses which grow out of a sloven's carelessness, in time, become almost incurable. Hence such people work like slaves, and to little effect.

OF INDUSTRY.

Q. What is industry?

A. It is a diligent attention to business in our several occupations.

Q. Is labor a curse or a blessing?

A. Hard labor or drudgery is often a curse, by making life toilsome and painful. But constant moderate labor is the greatest of blessings.

Q. Why then do people complain of it?

A. Because they do not know the evils of *not* laboring. Labor keeps the body in health, and makes men relish all their enjoyments. "The sleep of the laboring man is sweet," so is his food. He walks cheerful and whistling about his field or his shop, and scarcely knows pain.—The rich and indolent first lose their health for want of action— They turn pale, their bodies are enfeebled, they lose their appetite for food and sleep, they yawn out a tasteless life of dulness, without pleasure, and often useless to the world.

Q. What are the other good effects of industry?

A. One effect is to procure an estate. Our Creator has kindly united our duty, our interest, and happiness; for the same labor which makes us healthy and cheerful,

An Easy Standard of Pronunciation.

gives wealth.—Another good effect of industry is, to keep men from vice. Not all the moral discourses ever delivered to mankind, have so much effect in checking the bad passions of men, in keeping order and peace, and maintaining moral virtue in society, as *industry Business* is a source of health, of prosperity, of virtue and obedience to law.

To make good subjects and good citizens, the first requisite is to educate every young person in some kind of business. The possession of millions should not excuse a young man from application to business ; and that parent or guardian who suffers his child or his ward to be bred in idleness, becomes accessary to the vices and disorders of society—He is guilty of " not providing for his household, and is worse than an infidel."

OF CHEERFULNESS.

Q. Is cheerfulness a virtue?

A. It doubtless is, and a moral duty to practice it.

Q. Can we be cheerful when we please?

A. In general it depends much on ourselves. We can often mold our tempers into a cheerful frame. We can frequent company and other objects calculated to inspire us with cheerfulness. To indulge an habitual gloominess of mind is weakness and sin.

Q. What are the effects of cheerfulness on ourselves?

A. Cheerfulness is a great preservative of health, over which it is our duty to watch with care. We have no right to sacrifice our health by the indulgence of a gloomy state of mind. Besides, a cheerful man will do more business, and do it better, than a melancholy one.

Q. What are the effects of cheerfulness on others?

A. Cheerfulness is readily communicated to others, by which means their happiness is increased. We are all influenced by sympathy, and naturally partake of the joys and sorrows of others.

Q. What effect has melancholy on the heart?

A. It hardens and benumbs it—It chills the warm affections of love and friendship, and prevents the exercise of the social passions. A melancholy person's life is all

An Easy Standard of Pronunciation.

night and winter. It is as unnatural as perpetual darkness and frost.

Q. What shall one do when overwhelmed with grief?

A. The best method of expelling grief from the mind, or of quieting its pains, is to change the objects that are about us ; to ride from place to place, and frequent cheerful company. It is our duty so to do, especially when grief sits heavy on the heart.

Q. Is it not right to grieve for the loss of our friends ?

A. It is certainly right; but we should endeavor to moderate our grief, and not suffer it to impair our health or to grow into a settled melancholy. The use of grief is to soften the heart and make us better. But when our friends are dead, we can render them no further service. Our duty to them ends, when we commit them to the grave; but our duty to ourselves, our families, and surviving friends, requires that we perform to them the customary offices of life. We should therefore remember our departed friends only to imitate their virtues; and not to pine away with useless sorrow.

Q. Has not religion a tendency to fill the mind with gloom?

A. True religion never has this effect. Superstition and false notions of God, often make men gloomy ; but true, rational piety and religion have the contrary effect. They fill the mind with joy and cheerfulness; and the countenance of a truly pious man should always wear a serene smile.

Q. What has Christ said concerning gloomy Christians?

A. He has pronounced them hypocrites ; and commanded his followers not to copy their sad countenances and disfigured faces ; but even in their acts of humiliation to " anoint their heads and wash their face." Christ intended by this, that religion does not consist in, nor require a monkish sadness and gravity ; on the other hand, he intimates that such *appearances* of sanctity are generally the marks of hypocrisy. He expressly enjoins upon his followers marks of cheerfulness. Indeed, the only true ground of perpetual cheerfulness is, a consciousness ever having done well, and an assurance of divine

HENRY STEELE COMMAGER, Professor of History and American Studies at Amherst College, was born in Pittsburgh, Pennsylvania, in 1902. After receiving his Ph.B., his M.A., and his Ph.D. from the University of Chicago, he taught history at New York University from 1926 until 1939 and at Columbia University from 1939 until 1956, when he joined the Amherst faculty. He has also served as Pitt Professor at Cambridge University and Harmsworth Professor at Oxford University. Professor Commager's writings include *Theodore Parker* (1936), *The American Mind* (1950), and *The Spirit of Seventy-Six* (with Richard B. Morris, 1958). He was chief consultant editor of *The Encyclopedia of American History* (1953) and is co-editor of *The New American Nation Series* (1954–).